P9-BZM-201

Breaking the Silence

The Kerry Bog Pony

By

Mary Denis Reidy

Picture by Jerry Mulvihill

Gentleness, tenacity, endurance, survival and love.

M & R
Publishing

The Hobby
(Kerry Bog Pony)

by: Mary Denis Reidy © 13th December 2003

Gentle, unassuming pony
Left with the burden
To carry and haul
The sustenance of life

Each sod of turf provides warmth
The fire … the nourishment
Without the aid of the Hobby
An impossible task

The countryside remains the same
The duties are different
No longer totally dependent
On the Hobby or the turf

What now?
Extinction the reward for service
No crown of glory
No preservation of dignity

The Hobby now grazes
In fields plentiful
Not forgotten but revered
Breed for enjoyment and lineage

Long service honoured
A place in history
The Hobby still kind -hearted
Wants only to please

Kerry will not forget
The gentle unassuming pony
Love, faithfulness and devotion
Symbols for centuries

Published by M & R Publishing

Front cover design and sketch drawings by Gerardine Sheridan, Artist

Back cover photograph by Michael Diggin

Poems by Jerry Mulvihill, Vincent Counihan & Mary Denis Reidy

Photographs provided by John Mulvihill and The Kerry Bog Pony Society

Information and history on Donkeys and Donkey Sanctuary
By Paddy Barrett, Manager of Donkey Sanctuary, Liscarroll

ISBN No 095409901X

Copies of this book have been deposited in the following:

The British Library
The Library of Trinity College, Dublin
The National Library of Scotland, Edinburgh
The National Library of Wales, Aberystwyth
The University Library, Cambridge
The Bodleian Library, Oxford

M & R Publishing
Caragh Bridge
Glenbeigh
Co. Kerry, Ireland
+353 669768701
e-mail harii@gofree.indigo.ie

Printed by Leinster Leader Ltd.
18/19 Main Street
Naas, Co Kildare, Ireland

Dedication

To my beautiful, brave and versatile Dinny

Special Mention

The support and love of my husband, John was the driving force in the will to persevere in my writing. His belief in me has made all things possible.

It is important to understand that something must be saved before it is taken from our midst. John Mulvihill, the members of the Kerry Bog Pony Society, our law-makers, our conservationists and the ordinary people have worked to restore the Hobby to his place in history. Without these many individuals, this book could never have been written and is a testament to all of them.

Thank you

A special thank you to all that have been instrumental in the compilation, editing and printing of this book. Excerpts from the travels and writings of many people have given the background for the journey of the Hobby. The list is a very long one and mention of everyone is impossible, but the gratitude is genuine.

The dramatist, novelist, poet and reconteur,
John B. Keane, (1928-2002)
tells of his delight upon his introduction to the Kerry Bog Pony.

The Kerry Bog Pony

The Kerry Bog Pony is a most unassuming little equine. He is totally without pretension, a rare enough attribute in the equine sphere. He is the genuine article beyond any doubt.

I have heard him described as an "adorable little creature" and "a great all-rounder" and when my old friend, John Mulvihill, introduced me to him on my way from Cahirciveen some years ago I knew I was in elegant company. He stood modestly to one side as John extolled his many virtues.

He belongs to Kerry and expecially to its more isolated and inaccessible parts where he thrives. He is the very soul of sure-footedness and reliability and like his human counterpart he'll eat almost anything.

To John Flynn, Head of the Blood-typing Department of Weatherbys Ireland, and to John Mulvihill of the Red Fox Inn we are all deeply indebted and to all the others no less who rallied behind the cause of the Kerry Bog Pony. He now takes his place among the true strains of the Equine World and may be justifiably venerated like the Kerry Cow, The Kerry Blue, The Kerry Diamond, the shy Kerry Lily of Derrynane and the Kerry Set.

Thank you John Mulvihill. Your long crusade is over.

John B. Keane

Folklorist, short story writer, poet, playwright, producer of plays, novelist, lecturer and ballad-maker, Bryan Mac Mahon, LL.D (1909-1998) writes to John Mulvihill, Kerry Bog Village, about his enthusiasm regarding the Kerry Bog Pony and the addition of an indigenous breed.

The Kerry Bog Pony

A letter from Bryan MacMahon, LL.D

Mr. John Mulvihill
Ballincleave
Glenbeigh
Co. Kerry

31st August 1997

Dear John
I note with clear and keenest interest your dedicated endeavour to secure an acknowledged identity for the Kerry Bog Pony, and drop you a line to encourage you in your quest – you and the Pony Society you represent.
The reference by Charles Smith is, I think, very important indeed. His history of Kerry is a landmark publication. I do not pretend to be able to interpret the Weatherby Report but there are experts available of course who will be able to weigh its place in the pattern of your undertakings.
Never lose sight of your goal: if the breed is to achieve the identity of being a separate breed of pony, you will have achieved status (for it) in the equine world as already accorded to the Kerry Blue in the canine world and to the Kerry Cow in the bovine world. Truly then we could possess a shamrock of indigenous breeds – cow, pony and terrier.
Cordial personal regards,
I wish your undertakings every success!

Sincerely indeed,
Bryan MacMahon

Patrick Houlihan is a local historian, journalist, author and museum curator of the old ways that make Killorglin unique. His critique about "Breaking the Silence" is written in his own unique style.

Having read the manuscript of "Breaking the Silence" by Mary Denis Reidy I was amazed by the amount of Irish history it contained. The purpose of the book was to prove the existence of the animal called the "Hobby" or "Bog Pony." This she proved in no uncertain manner. When rural Ireland was destitute their only possessions were perhaps a dog, a few foul and a small sturdy pony that dragged the sled with its hard won peat from the nearby bogs.

This peat generated heat and comfort for the harsh winters of past centuries. The "Hobby" and the Bogs of Ireland became synonymous and now its wonderful story and history of this useful and loveable animal is to be made available in book form.

In writing this, Mary Denis is taking the reader through many ages of distant Irish history. She cites the "Spanish Armada" wrecked on the Kerry coast and wonders if the first Hobby's swam ashore and got established here in the South. She also mentions the Great Rebellion of 1641, the penal laws, the tyrant Oliver Cromwell, King James of 1685, and the insurrection of 1798 and the effect that those upheavals had on the Irish people.

During all this time everyday life had to go on as people made do with what was available. One sure resource was the vast expanse of bog land and their sturdy and faithful Hobby, who was forever at their service.

Today, to see the Bog Pony at his most beautiful best, one must visit the Kerry Bog Village at Quay Bawn.

These animals are daily admired by thousands of visitors from many lands.

In conclusion, I wish the best of luck to Mary Denis in compiling and publishing another masterpiece to add to her past literary gems

Forward

Written by
Professor Brendan Kennelly

Heroes come in all shapes and sizes. Some are tall and handsome, some small and squat. Some are human, some are not. This book by Mary Denis Reidy is a delightful, informative and at times deeply moving account of a very special hero – the Kerry Bog Pony, or the Hobby, as he is known.

The book's title, Breaking the Silence, is aptly chosen. For far too long, the heroic contribution of the Hobby to the survival of the Kerry people during times of impoverishment and oppression went unrecognised and uncelebrated. But now, thanks to people like John Mulvihill and John Flynn, and to this gripping book by Mary Denis Reidy, the heroic Hobby has come into his own.

"Breaking the Silence" is powered by a deep desire to see justice done to a brave and noble creature, the Kerry Bog Pony. I believe that readers of this book will agree that the story of the Hobby has at last been told with knowledge, energy and precision.

In telling this remarkable story, Mary Denis Reidy has done some helpful historical research and tells us, in clear language, how the Hobby came to Ireland. She also gives us another history, equally fascinating in its way – the history, and indeed the geography, of the Irish bogs, at once fertile and treacherous. The Hobby worked hard in the bogs, coping with hidden dangers, bringing home the turf that enabled poor families to survive very cold bitter winters.

Mary Denis Reidy tells this revealing, moving story with a kind of simple, detached elegance. Her style captures many different aspects of the lives of deprived and victimised people helped by a great-hearted pony, a trojan worker, an uncompromising reliable friend of people in need.

Readers will, I believe, thoroughly enjoy this tale of a small, sturdy hero being accorded the honour he richly deserves.

Preface

The Kerry Bog Pony can be traced from the early 1700's through the writings of many noted travellers to the Kerry countryside. Among them is M. Tournfort, Isaac Ware, Charles Smith's "Natural and Civic History of Kerry" (published in 1756), Elwyn Hartley's "The Encyclopedia of the Horse", Professor E Estyn Evans' Irish Folkways" William Lighgow, Elwyn Hartley Edwards, Professor David Low, R. S. Summerhays' "The Observers Book of Horses and Ponies", Mr. John Mulvihill, President of the Kerry Bog Pony Society and initiator of the movement to establish and place the Kerry Bog Pony in Equine History, Mr. Daniel Hutch, Veterinary Surgeon, John Flynn, head of the Blood typing department of Weatherbys, Dr Leo Curran, Lecturer at U.C.D., Mr. Michael Del Las Cassas, Rare Breed Society and many others that have authenticated the Hobby as a breed of pony existing in the mountains and bogs of Kerry.

This book "Breaking the Silence" uses the information from these various sources and initiates a story of the Hobby as he might have or did exist among the people of Kerry. The book takes the reader from the Spanish Armada through to the modern times of 2004 and makes it possible to imagine the journey of this humble pony and his effects on the lives and hopes of a nation enduring throughout the impossible. Whether the Hobby actually made the trip, as outlined in this book, is imaginative but not untrue. It is entirely possible that the rebellions, wars, poverty, penal laws, faith, superstitions and eventual recognition are a part of the Hobby's history. It is certain that he existed and is a breed unto himself.

The stories of the Hobby persisted in the face of times long past in the annals of Irish History. In the modern day, there is little evidence of the hardship of this land and the suffering of its people. It is now the land of the 'Celtic Tiger' and all that phrase has come to connote. The landscape of old houses, poor people and despicable conditions are notes in history books for the well-educated children of Ireland to read and study. With the technology of today, storytelling is not the same medium as in the past. The media now glamorises occurrences, which fade as quickly as a new fetish catches the imagination of the people. As each upcoming generation passes the torch to the next, the many gifts of the past become lost in the transmission.

Fortunately, love of land, animals and the lifestyle of old and new Ireland has been perpetuated and kept due to the vigilance of those sentimental and sturdy people who believe that'we are our past.' The future depends on remembering and preserving heritage and custom.

"Breaking the Silence" is not a history book, definitive account of the past or authoritative documentation of Ireland's evolution into the twenty-first century. Rather, it is a story to be enjoyed and contemplated. The trek from the seventeenth century to 1994 is partly substantiated and partly romanticised. From the second half of the 1990s, the finding of a stallion and a few mares is fact beyond dispute. The Hobby had survived and was rescued by a group of people dedicated to his furtherance. John Mulvihill, a realist and dreamer, chanced upon 'an old pony' and the rest became part of the resurgence of the Hobby. From there, the Hobby has been bloodtyped, researched, nourished and now revealed. The Kerry Bog Pony Society, the specialists that have investigated and specified and finally the love, all have contributed to this book. But, more importantly the 'gift of the Kerry Bog Pony' affectingly known as the Hobby is now part of Irish heritage.

Contents

Chapter 1

The silence is deafening. The stark countryside of Kerry is quiet and in whispers. Each day is a chore that demands more resilience than the ordinary man and woman in the South West of Ireland can endure, but must endure. Their voices and their desires are silent because of domination. Their lives are ruled by poverty, lack of education in any formal sense and the overwhelming torment of subservience.

Outside the humble door rests the few animals that are permitted under the system in which the people live. Among them is the small pony that allows for some measure of comfort in their lives. Few of the Kerry farmers in the middle of the 17th century would have taken the time or thought process to ascertain if their pony could be determined as pure stock. Their only concern was centred in the drawing of peat from the bog to keep the chill and winds from overcoming their health. This same God-given animal helped them to haul seaweed from the oceanfront to provide nourishment to their modest crops. It was amazing that the pony had adapted to the deprivation of his masters. The Kerry Bog Pony, as he became known, could dine on whatever was available leaving the other small provisions the farmer had to accommodate the few livestock that he was fortunate enough to possess.

Not everyone had the small pony that could traverse the bogs.

They were in moderate numbers due to the dwindling stock that had been transported for pack animals during the Peninsular wars. They were not distinctive enough to be of any real value to the current rulers of the land. Long ago, the horses had been commandeered for use by the army or the hunt, which was a popular sport engaged in by the ruling class. Each pony, although owned by one family, was used by the entire community and worked without complaint. They could be seen in the boglands of Dingle, Killarney, Kenmare, Listowel, Tralee and most of the remote mountainous areas. They worked, alongside their owner for the day, from early morning to late night carrying the turf.

The bogs were extremely wet and precarious places to traverse. Every step could mean that the pony and farmer might be stuck in a hole making the process of cutting and drawing much more difficult. The pony, powerfully built with good bone and weight relative to its size, is sure-footed and capable of thinking for itself in the soft underfoot conditions of the bogs.

Ingenuity and determination necessitated that the Kerry Bog pony be used to best advantage. With the passage of time many meth-

ods were devised to allow for better manipulation of these animals affectionately called the 'Hobby.' Lightweight types of harnesses were developed to attach to slides allowing for the Hobby to pull the laden baskets of turf successfully across the slippery surfaces of the bog. The Hobby was able to draw sufficient load permitting the timely excavation of turf for the needs of many families.

Common sense demanded that the farmers of Kerry maintain this breed of pony, which was providing invaluable service with so little maintenance. It became incumbent upon them to preserve and foster the existence of the Hobby. Somehow, through the whispers, they were able to connect with each other and breed this pony allowing for its preservation and their own. It must have been within the system of sharing the Hobby that it was able to carry on. Probably, it was not in the true nature of making pure stock that the breed was kept, but in the desire to endure in a land that was harsh.

In addition to its work ethics, the Hobby was an endearing animal in temperament and appearance. He provided the farmer and his family with a mode of transportation because of the incredible strength contained within such a small structure. Most of the Hobbies are only 10 to 12 hands in height. Their dished or carved faces are distinctive and friendly. There is an air of bravery mixed with sadness in their demeanour. Their colouring is predominately chestnut with black, grey or possibly bay mane and tail. Their coat is long and dense allowing for their sustenance in harsh weather conditions outdoors without shelter.

It is difficult to state the disposition of this small pony. Many animals, like people, become crabby when the day's labour is too long and hard. Possibly, it is because the Hobby possesses the physical condition of large heart and lung capacity, that his temperament remains in sound condition while undertaking enormous tasks. Whatever the demand, the beginning and the end, the Hobby was the same gentle animal. He seemed to delight in the pleasure of the

labour well done and was ready and able to continue until the demand of the day was over.

Man and animal are interchangeable in the annals of history. Living conditions, tradition and the exchange of stories sustain the need to develop and nurture some strong symbol of existence. The Hobby became such an obligation.

Whether he kept the spirit of free thought and joy alive over the centuries for the Kerry people is to be determined. All stories, including those of the Gospel, were fables passed from one person to another until they were written for all to read and hear. The method of history is in the writing and recording. The Hobby deserves his day and his story is one that will span the centuries from the 1700's to the current day. By the preservation of this wonderful small pony will history be told and the dedication of man revealed.

Chapter 2

The years of the latter part of the sixteenth century played a large part in the history of Spain, England and Ireland. In that time-frame, the King of Spain, Philip II, decided to claim superiority of the Seas and bring the nation of England back to the true faith. In doing so, Phillip II would also ensure that Spain remain the only force to govern on the seas. England was gaining in its efforts to overcome Spain's supremacy.

History tells of the brutal defeat of the Spanish fleet, commanded by the Duke of Medina Sedonia. After losing many ships to the English, the Duke decided to forego the invasion and return to Spain via the coast of Scotland and Ireland. The Armada was badly damaged and pursued by the English for many days. Several of the ships had to go aground on the coasts of Scotland and Ireland.

It might have been in the floundering of these ships that the Hobby was first introduced to Kerry. An architect, Isaac Ware, travelled throughout Kerry in 1720 and noted for record that he believed that the Hobby was a descendant of a Spanish pony called Austuriones, which was imported from Austurias, Spain. Some believe that the Hobby might have been a part of the Armada for use after the conquest of England to carry goods over the terrain. The influence of the Spanish Armada on the coast of Ireland can be seen in the complexion of some of the people in Kerry. It has been said that a dark eyed beauty living on a farm in the remotest part of the mountains carries the mark of that fatal time in the Spanish History. The destruction of the fleet was Spain's loss and Ireland's gain. Whether the Hobby came ashore as a result of the

GETTING TO SHORE FROM A SHIPWRECK
SPANISH SAILORS
POSSIBLE SOURCE OF PONIES

partial casualty of a fleet or was imported in some other way from Spain is very uncertain. Either way, the Hobby became an intrical part in the weaving of the lives and habits of the local people of Ireland, particularly Kerry. He evolved into a very important component in the lives of the poor and overworked.

It is important to understand the environment into which the Hobby first emerged. It was a land that had lost its privilege to have any decision making voice. For many centuries, the Irish had elected a landlord or king. This persisted throughout the twelfth century when Dermot Mac Murrough invited Norman mercenaries to help him with his local problems. What was considered a problem was the fact that the Irish were a people that wished freedom and revolted against authority with habitual regularity. By the year 1640, 35% of all tillable land in Ireland was owned by invaders or English soldiers/settlers.

In 1641 the Irish mounted a nation-wide war known as the 'Great Rebellion.' It dragged on for eleven years and ended with the appearance of Oliver Cromwell to squash the rebellion. He marched on some Irish cities and proceeded to kill all in his path. When the war was over in 1652, there was only one-third of the Irish Catholic population left with additional thousands being transported to the West Indies to work as slaves. The reward for this service was large tracks of Irish land making the total of land owned by Irish a mere 25% in the wake of this rebellion. In spite of all this, it was said, "an Irish nation still existed…separate, numerous and hostile.' Because of the savagery of Cromwell and his destruction of land and people, the English believed that the Irish rebellions were a thing of the past. They were wrong.

New thoughts of rebellion started again when the Irish thought they found a champion for the restoration of their lands. Charles II, King of England died and was succeeded by King James in 1685. James was Catholic and the Irish believed that he would be sympathetic to their plight. They threw all their support behind James, but the Protestants of England would not allow James to prosper. They invited William of Orange to contest James' reign and in 1688 William defeated James.

James fled to France and mounted a counter-attack. His strategy

was to first gain a beachhead in Ireland where he knew he had overwhelming support. In 1690, he was again defeated by William of Orange at the Battle of the Boyne.

Even though the English were victorious, they wanted to put in place laws that would prohibit the Irish Catholics from being a threat on an island so close to the shore of England. It was at that time that the English enacted the Penal Laws which forbade the Irish from obtaining any form of education, serving in the military, all professional vocations, any civic responsibilities, attending Catholic church service, purchasing land and owning a horse valued at £5 or more. They were required to pay tithe to the Church

of England, which added insult to injury. The population of Ireland, in the later 1600's was 95% Catholic. The ministers of the Church of England received large sums of money for support of their churches from people that would not and did not attend their services.

The Hobby did not qualify as a horse or pony that was worth more than £5 and was therefore a Godsend to the farmers and herders of this rule-laden land. Without the efforts of this humble animal, there would be no help for the hauling and transport in some of the harshest conditions known to man.

The Penal Laws had accomplished their expected results. Within a few generations, the Catholic Irish were reduced to abject poverty, were illiterate (or nearly so) and unskilled. In 1750, 93% of land was owned by non-Irish landowners and by 1770 it was practically 100%. The Irish had become a nation of tenant farmers. Visitors from other parts of Europe noted that the Irish peasant was poorer than the lowest serfs in Poland and Germany. Their lives were ones of desperation and deprivation. Almost half of the population lived in small windowless mud cabins. Furniture con-

sisted of a bed and some chairs...and only a very few had such luxuries.

It was normal for farm animals, pigs and chickens, to sleep in the cabin with the people. However, the good news was that the huts were always warm in the winter thanks to the readily available peat and the use of the Hobby to transport the turf from the bog to the huts. The people were poor and destitute, but as usual were thankful and rebellious at the same time. Whatever few animals they possessed were treated with dignity and gratitude. The Hobby was well cared for under the circumstances. He demanded little in the way of food provided by the tenant farmers. He maintained good spirit in spite of deplorable conditions for himself and his owners. He was so adaptable to his current conditions that his numbers multiplied. It was amazing that the Hobby started to be seen in large numbers on the countryside of Kerry and his services were used by almost every tenant farmer. At this time in Irish history, the tenant farmers were living on sometimes less than one acre of land. The landlords had seen a way to increase their rental income by dividing and sub-dividing their land resulting in double the rent paid by Irish tenant farmers than their counterparts in England.

There was a constant atmosphere of rebellion that arose as a result of the inhuman laws and regulations placed on a proud people. In 1760, another plan went into motion, which became known as the 'Whiteboys.' Their sole objective was to tear down fences, hamstring cattle and burn barns of the landlords. They punished informers in a terrible form of revenge. They rode to manor houses destroying property and shooting through the windows. The landlords feared the retribution of the 'Whiteboys' and lived in permanently barricaded houses guarded by teams of sentries.

The Irish used this tactic and worked to organise another war strategy, which became known as the Insurrection of 1798. They were to revolt simultaneously all over Ireland with the help of a

1798 – MASSACRE OF PIKEMEN

large force of French soldiers. The French army ran into a severe storm and most of the ships sank leaving the Irish to carry out the revolt unaided. They possessed only pikes and clubs against Loyalist soldiers with muskets and canon. At Vinegar Hill in County Wexford they were defeated and the common comment was that "they fell like new mown grass." This insurrection was met without mercy and thousands were butchered while on their knees begging for mercy. More Irish were killed in the aftermath retaliation than in the actual battles.

Chapter 3

The bogs of the seventeenth and eighteenth centuries were of a quality that is not present in modern times. The peat contained in the bog is made up of the partially decomposed remains of dead plants, which have accumulated on top of each other in waterlogged places for thousands of years. These areas are called peat lands and are comprised of a brownish-black substance composed of 90% water and 10% solid material. They consist of Sphagnum

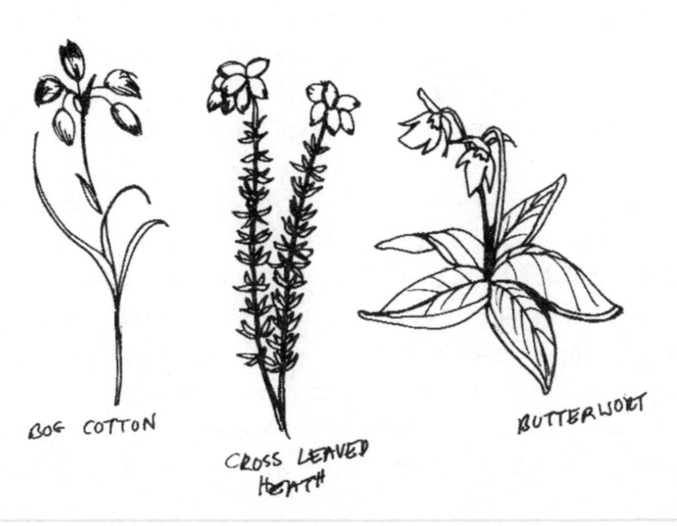

moss along with the roots, leaves, flowers and seeds of heather, grasses and sedges. Occasionally, the trunks and roots of trees such as Scots pine, oak, birch and yew are also present in the peat.

There are two types of peat land found in Ireland; fens and bogs.
The fens and bogs are similar and different. The fens are alkaline while the bogs are acid, both are waterlogged, fens are mineral rich while bogs are mineral poor, fens have a high ash content while bogs are low in ash content and the depth of the fen is up to 2m. with the bog depth varying from 2m. to 12m.

The bogs can be further distinguished by characterising the differences between raised and blanket bogs. The blanket bogs can be differentiated again by the Atlantic blanket bog (below 200m) and the mountain bog (above 200m). The raised bogs are found in the midlands of Ireland because the rainfall is less than the blanket bogs found along the West Coast or in mountainous area where rainfall is greater.

Raised bog formation started at the end of the last glaciation, some 10,000 years ago. The glaciers retreated north which left central Ireland covered by shallow lakes; the residuals of the melting ice. The water was trapped disabling free drainage and creating lakes fed by mineral-rich groundwater, which supported plant communities producing thin layers of peat. In time the peat layer in these shallow lakes became so thick that the roots of plants growing on the surface were no longer in contact with the calcium-rich

groundwater. The plants present were able to survive allowing for their source of minerals coming solely from rainwater.
This made for vastly changing conditions, which invited the invasion of bog moss making the ground more acid. This began the intermediate stage between fen and bog. The bog moss is important because it acts as a sponge keeping the bog wet and waterlogged even in the driest periods. Even though the bog continued

to grow upward, away from the water table, the Bog Moss ensured that the water table rose in tandem with the rising peat level.
In the 17th and 18th centuries the peat in the bogs was very waterlogged and difficult to traverse. The period from the melting of the glaciers to that timeframe was insufficient to allow for the water tables to diminish to the current day. For the tenant farmers to cut, stook and remove the turf from the bogs of Kerry was a time-consuming and difficult task. The bogs were very wet on the surfaces making it hard to bring the turf to the huts where the farmers lived. Almost anything would sink into the soft surface because of the excess amount of water.
The Hobby was built in a way that allowed him to carry the sled and turf out to the homes without much difficulty. He was surefooted and seemed to have the ability to understand the places to

avoid. His structure was sturdy while his needs were small. He worked from dawn to dusk without complaint, feeding only on the plants and trees provided in the bog. It is unlikely that the wild

landscape, rugged beauty and colouration of the bogs were much noticed by the people of Kerry in past centuries. Their main concern was to keep the huts warm and their families free of disease in the cold and windy weather of winter.

Many plants are commonly found in the Irish bogs. A core of species includes Ling Heather, Cross-leaved Heath, Bog Cotton,

Sundew, Bog Bean, Bog Asphodel, White Beak Sedge and a large number of Bog Mosses or Sphagnum Mosses. The common factor in these plants is that they can survive in mineral-poor soil. Large portions of these plants are edible and were the main source of nourishment for the Hobby.

Due to the rigid and harsh living conditions imposed at this time in history, every tool available was utilised by the farmers/herders. The Bog Wood was used for cutlery and farm utensils carved by the farmers with very crude materials. Some of these objects were hand crafted from peat itself or from the bog wood. The peat and bog wood was used by people in the field of the arts in the endeavour of making cards, jewellery and ornamented harps.

As the rules of the English landlords became harder and harder the value of the Hobby became more apparent. There was little to recommend life in these hard times, but the heat from turf was a small luxury that the farmers had. It was the Hobby, in large part that made that possible. Like the people, the Hobby had adapted to the conditions in which he lived. Because of this adaptability, he was a treasured and invaluable animal to do the work.

The bogs were intricately involved with the people of the time becoming a major part of the existence of the farmers and herders. Like the Hobby, stories, songs and poems were written to foster remembrance. Vincent Counihan, poet, wrote of the beauty of the bogs and the lonely virtue of their vastness. His voice is in the present day, but it echoes the sentiments of the past mingled with all that the peat bogs represented to the people.

The Bogs of Ireland

The bogs of Ireland are a lonely site
To pass upon a cold cold winter's night
But thinking back across years long since gone
You see the once fine setting for a song
For there, there grew the Elm and the Yew with Fox Gloves bearing pearls of morning dew
And birds who sang a song so sweet and true to humour fairies dancing in the morning dew.
©Vincent Counihan 1966

TURF-CUTTER 1800s

Chapter 4

To the end of the eighteenth century, the Hobby thrived and multiplied becoming the mainstay for collection of turf from the bogs, transportation for the farmers and nourishment from the sea for the crops. It was most likely that the Hobby was noticed by the rulers of Ireland as a willing and strong beast of burden who required little to maintain. For this reason, and the fact that the Hobby's numbers were sufficient to deplete, they were commandeered for use by the armies fighting the Peninsular Wars. Again, the poor tenant farmers/herders were to be deprived of one of the mainstays of their existence. The task of heating was made bearable because of the Hobby. Without him, even warmth would be almost unattainable.

The Peninsular Wars were a series

of engagements between France and a number of European nations from the years 1799 to 1815. There were many fazes to the wars that included the details of multiple coalitions ranging from the first to the fourth. The nations that were engaged in this conflict were varied and sometimes continuous from the first coalition to the fourth. Great Britain, Spain, Prussia, Kingdom of Sardinia, Austria, Egypt, Portugal, Ottoman Empire, Russia and the Kingdom of Naples all engaged Napoleon during multiple or individual aspects of the conflict.

The Peninsular Wars were in essence a continuation of the French Revolution (1789-1799) and were engaged into in an effort to return France to the rule of the monarch and to dissolve the revolutionary government of France.

Given the expanse of territory that engaged in the war effort, it is not surprising that the Hobby was deemed a pony of preference for the transport of heavy artillery in the remotest parts of Italy and in the dessert conditions of Egypt. The English were the most probable nation to introduce the benefits of the Hobby because of their awareness of his abilities from the exploits of Isaac Ware's travels and the account written in 1756, in the work of Charles

Smith's "Natural and Civic History of Kerry." Charles Smith wrote of the Hobby "The little Hobbies of the country are the most correct horses to travel through it; and a man must abandon himself entirely to their guidance, which will answer much better than if one should strive to manage and direct their footsteps; for these creatures are a kind of automata, or machines, as M. Toumfort has long since observed, which naturally follow the laws of mechanics, and will conduct themselves much better on those occasions, than the most knowing persons can possibly direct them."

During the Peninsular Wars, given the information written about them, it is not a far assumption that the Hobby was used by the English army to haul their artillery and men in the mountainous areas of Austria, Spain, Italy and many other countries. The ponies caused little inconvenience to the men of the army and were used as food when the supplies ran low or out. They were able to forage on whatever was available thereby not using any of the rations that they had to transport. Their surefootedness in the mountains of foreign nations was a legacy from the mountains of their origins in Kerry. Their body structure and heavy winter coats allowed them to trudge through the Alps in the harshest of conditions without shelter. They were greatly diminished in numbers because their value was not appreciated except for carry and haul and as a last resort, food.

It must be supposed that some of the Hobbies survived the years of the Peninsular Wars and placed their mark on the countries in which they travelled. It is difficult to imagine that, considering the number of Hobbies that were transported that none survived and multiplied. Maybe in the end, they became one of the helpers of the poor farmers in the countries of Spain, Italy, Austria and others. They might have come full cycle in the years of 1799 to 1815 in that they returned to their origins in Spain, if indeed they were originally descended from that country.

Largely, the countries of Europe share many of the same ingredients because of the saga of assault throughout the centuries. It is not impossible to envision that the Hobby might have been introduced, at first, by the Romans and than reinforced by further inva-

sions at other periods in history. Whatever their first introduction to the Irish people, they became the sustenance of many of the mountainous regions.

The Peninsular Wars seriously damaged the chances of the Hobby. Their numbers were hopelessly depleted. They went to the mountains of Kerry for survival and succour. It was in these mountain ranges that the fate of the Hobby was preserved. The farmer needed the Hobby for life-sustenance as much as the Hobby needed the farmer for care and love. Each fulfilled the other, but the Hobby did not roam the harsh terrain of Kerry freely anymore. The little pony had to be safeguarded. Transportation of additional numbers could not be tolerated.

Chapter 5

The people of Ireland somehow survived the ordeals of the uprising, Cromwell, the Peninsular Wars and had augumented their population. They had expanded to a nation of over eight million by the middle eighteen hundreds. It is true that they had little or no rights under the penal laws and systems of the time, but they had their faith and superstitions to comfort them.

There was a very long history of Christianity from the time of St. Patrick in the beginning of the first century AD with the subsequent conversion of the people to that faith. The story of St. Patrick was told and retold around the fires in the impoverished homes of the people. It was recanted time and again how Patrick (originally named Succat) was probably born in south western Britain and was carried off at sixteen years of age by Irish marauders to pass his captivity as a herdsman near the mountain Slemish in county Antrim or in Connacht. They believed that Patrick saw visions divining that he escape, which he did after six years in slavery. He became a priest in the Christian faith and returned to Ireland concentrating his missionary efforts mostly in the West. He became the Bishop of Ireland and is noted for his conversion of the pagan Irish to the true faith. The people of Kerry held these anecdotes dear to the hearth because it was personal to their history since Patrick spent time in their area. The symbol of the Shamrock prevailed as a sign of the Trinity that was God the Father, Son and Holy Spirit.

Before the advent of St. Patrick, the Irish were invaded with regularity and embraced the habits and ways of the conquerors. The stories and fables persisted within the maze of belief in the true faith of St. Patrick. The narrative of the Celts and the Druids were the fodder that feed the imaginations of the young and oppressed. In the small comfort of the mud huts, the storytellers recounted the history of the Druids with their pagan gods and goddesses. It was told how the Celt language was rarely used, but was replaced by oral tradition to relay the religious and philosophical beliefs of those days. This was a ritual that was being perfected in the countryside of Ireland.

The gods of worship within the Druid society were replaced as saints by the conversion to Christianity. The seventh century sent the Druids underground due to the pressure of the Christian forces. This did not stop the furtherance of the people and their fascination with the powers of superstition. From the Druids, the Irish peasant divined a powerful respect for the use of fire and the fascination with the number three. The bonfires that became a mark of the Druid tradition were a symbol that was embraced and

continued for centuries after the Druids lost control to Christianity.

There was no lack of verbal warnings concerning positive or negative foreboding in a land devoid of little but dreams. For generations the legends of the fairies keep the fancy of the mind in a state of awareness to the good and evil that was always present among the poor.

There was a medley of fairies to engage the fear and anticipation of the people. Children and adults alike went to sleep on many occasions thinking and then dreaming about the powers of the different fairies that dwelt among them.

The Leprechaun was one of the most popular of the fairies because he was considered a shoemaker and could be found in an intoxicated state due to the use of the home-brew poteen. He was believed to be the protector and self-appointed guardian of ancient treasure, which was left by the Danes when they plundered through Ireland. The imaginative minds in the countryside of Ireland believed that the Leprechaun was unsociable because he did not trust the people whom he considered to be foolish, flighty and greedy. From the cradle to the grave, there were few that did not wish for the pot of gold that the Leprechaun possessed and even fewer who believed that they could not, somehow, outwit this simple fairy. He had built in devices to deceive the seekers. He possessed two coins, which he would give them when they were able to capture him. One of the coins, however, would return to his purse after he was freed and the other would turn to leaves or ashes. Even so, most of the people still thought they could outsmart the Leprechaun.

The variety and veracity of the fairies was unlimited. The Banshee was to forewarn members of a household when someone was to die. Their skill was limited to specific households and the Banshee

would cry only for members of those families. The Changelings were the fairies that would substitute themselves for a healthy, beautiful baby born to a family and then cause no amount of havoc to that family. Once the baby was substituted, there was no prosperity or peace for the family that was in possession of the Changelings. They would be drained of all good fortune. Those chosen for the change were normally poor and were reduced to desperate struggle in order to maintain the ravenous monster in their midst. The redeeming factor in the household of the Changeling was the pure sound of perfectly played music. These, otherwise hindrances, had a musical aptitude second to none. It was said that they could play any instrument to perfection on the first introduction.

Other members of the fairy kingdom were the Grogoch, the Pooka and the Dullaghan. The Grogoch was a half-human, half fairy aborigine who resembled a very small elderly man, covered in coarse, reddish hair or fur with no clothing. He had the power of invisibility and would only appear when he trusted the people. He was sociable and helped with domestic and planting chores. He feared clergymen and could be dispensed, if he became a nuisance, by inviting a member of the church to dinner.

Many stories are told of the various fairies by the people of Kerry. There is one in particular that extols the virtues and fears of the Grogoch. A young woman, Mary, was to be wed to a farmer/herder in the mountain region of Kenmare. Mary was very young and her husband to be, John, was in his middle years at the time of their marriage. In the house where Mary was raised, every precaution was taken to keep the hut free of fairies and their unwanted effects on the family. Mary was reared in the atmosphere of superstition and omens.

After her marriage, Mary sensed the presence of a being in her new home but did not speak of her sensations for fear of ridicule by John and his family. It was already a broad topic of conversation in the family circle concerning the background of Mary's family.

Each night, after all the chores were done, Mary would sit at the hearth and watch the dying embers. She always went to the marriage bed and did her duty, but left as soon as she heard the snoring and deep sleep of John.

This situation continued for the fifteen years of the marriage until John fell and was badly hurt. Mary called the priest and shortly afterward John died. Mary was left to rear their nine children with the help of her brothers, but was a different person after the death of her husband. She told all that would listen, that the fairy had left the house when John died and she was able to sleep in her own bed without fear.

Whereas the Grogoch was a helpful fairy in his way, the Pooka was a fairy to be feared because he was always out after dark creating harm and mischief and had the ability to assume a variety of terrifying forms. He demanded a share of crops, prevented cows from milking and hens from laying. Horrific stories accompanied all tales about the Pooka.

Another of the fairies, perhaps one of the most spectacular creatures, is the Dullaghan. He rides a horse and is headless. He carries his head allowing for light in darkness because his head glows with the phosphorescence of decaying matter and the creature uses it as a lantern. When the Dullaghan appears, he calls out a name. The name of the person he calls always dies.

POOKA

Faith and sustenance are synonymous in most instances, but not always. When the time is rebellious, freedom denied, education forbidden, amenities of life withheld, sometimes faith must be mingled with fantasy.

The stories of history, fairies and St. Patrick were the stuff that fuelled the fires of the hearts of the people of Kerry. As the years rolled by and the hardship remained constant, new fables and symbols came into fashion. By the telling, over and over, do the newer adages take precedence over the old? Each small goodness is met with a story of greatness and is taken out of prospective in some instances. The Hobby became such a fable. He was real, worked for his masters and carried his load, but because he was taken in great numbers from the poor, he became legend in his own right. After the depletion in the Peninsular Wars, the fervour of saving the Hobby was burnt into the souls of the people of Kerry. Stories of his valour, labour and faithfulness became the fuel for story-telling and the need to preserve the Hobby's lineage, a passion.

Chapter 6

Ireland is a land that has undergone thousands of years of history. Each decade from the recording of time is indicative of the tempest in a teapot that formed the foundations of the Irish temperament. The earliest pre-history of Ireland is passed down in the

form of saga stories, legal tracts, annalistic records and fragmentary accounts which were recorded centuries after they actually may have occurred. Because of this type of record keeping, most scholars discount much of the accounts from pre-Christian and early Christian Ireland. Some very ancient chronicles, 'Annals of the Four Masters' include stories of ancient tribes whose arrival outdated the invasion of the Gael. The tribal history is sketchy at best

attempting to detail the various positions of the invaders and their roll in the formation of Ireland. The earliest (assumed) settlers arrived in Ireland in the year 10,000 BC. They crossed by land bridge from Scotland and were mainly hunters.
By the year 3000BC, colonists of the Neolithic, or new stone-age period reached Ireland. These people were farmers leaving rem-

nants of their civilisation, which has been excavated in Co. Limerick. They traded in a limited form of products, such as axe-heads. One of their monuments is a megalithic tomb at Newgrange in Co. Meath.

2000BC saw the advent of prospectors and metalworkers giving rise to the creation of bronze and gold objects. Some examples of the Bronze Age experience have been found in the form of axe-heads, pottery and jewellery.

In 600 BC the Celts arrived from central Europe. They continued their migration until the beginning of Christianity. In the time-frame between 600BC and the time of St. Patrick, the Celts dominated Ireland defeating the tribes already resident on the island. It is described that the Celtic language can be variously placed in a large window, but it is generally accepted that it was established between the Celt arrival and 500 years. There was little unity under the Celts with the exception of culture and language. The land was divided among five kings in provinces. There was a simple agrarian economy where no coins were used and the cow was the unit of exchange.

There are many accounts from authors such as T.F. O'Rahilly's book "Early Irish History and Mythology" and D. J. Conway's Ancient and Shining Ones" which put forth validity to many of these happenings. Written history became acceptable in the time of 461AD when the events of St. Patrick's introduction and conversion of the Irish people was recorded. By 800AD the island was attacked by the Viking Norsemen where they made established settlements in Waterford, Dublin and Limerick. The Vikings were defeated by Brian Boru in 1002 AD giving him recognition as King of all Ireland. There were a series of Kings for Ireland, which continued until the English conquered Ulster as well as Connacht and Munster in 1272AD. In the early 1300s Edward Bruce of Scotland invaded Ireland but failed in his attempt to overthrow the Norman Rule. By the mid-century of 1300 an edict banning pure-blooded Irish from becoming mayors, bailiffs, officers of the king or clergymen, or serving the English was posted.

By the 15th century, King Henry VIII of England had a breach with Rome and established himself as head of the Church of England. He also declared himself King of Ireland. His many successors demanded the cessation of the Catholic Faith in Ireland leading to anarchy. By the end of the century, the events of the Spanish Armada and their effects on the Irish countryside are recorded. The Hobby could have participated in the floundering of the Spanish Fleet or have been a part of previous invasions. Because the reconstruction of ancient events is so sketchy with regard to humans, there is little or no mention of the animals that assisted in those times. As with all of Irish history, much is lost or given little credence due to the conical method.

Turmoil and advancement became the outcome of the various forces that made their mark on the Irish Island. History, whether written or passed by fable over the centuries, relay the turbulent and unsettled nature of the peoples that invaded and inhabited Ireland. There is no wonder that such engrossing changes and innovations would give rise to the tradition of preserving heritage by the spoken word. As the progressive invaders imposed their will on a land that was already saturated by change, tradition had to be held in some form.

Chapter 7

The Peninsular Wars brought increased prosperity to the Irish landlords due to the demand for agricultural products. When the war ended, the need for these products decreased dramatically. To

compensate for the loss of revenue, the landlords decided to turn their lands into grazing and evict the resident tenant farmers to achieve their goal. In the first quarter of that century, large numbers could be seen of these wretched people wandering aimlessly, begging for food to keep alive.

The Irish proved rebellious to this outrage and created more secret societies to harass and carry out midnight raids resulting in further punishment of transportation of Irish. This episode took the offenders to Australia for seven years to life, depending on the severity of the crime. Any small theft would demand at least seven years.

In some ways the eviction of the tenant farmers and the conversion of the lands to grazing proved beneficial to the Hobby. His numbers were scarce after the war. He was overused to a degree of necessity by the large amount of tenant farmers in the Kerry region. When the landlords converted the lands, the Hobby was able to retreat to the mountains and multiply enabling its numbers to increase. He lacked the care, however limited, that he had received from the families he had helped to keep warm. His service was still used by the farmers that were not dispossessed allowing for his lineage furtherance both on the farm and in the mountains.

Deprivation and punishment can deprive the soul of desire to continue the effort to survive. This was not the case of the Irish. In addition to the loss of their lands, paramount in the eyes of the Irish land lovers, the potato crop failed in the middle of the 19th century. In 1845 blight struck the potato crop and half of the crop was destroyed. People husbanded what few potatoes they had and prayed that the next year's crop would be a bountiful one. The crop of 1846 suffered even more than the previous year. To add to the misery, that winter was the 'severest in living memory.' When the 1847 crop failed also, the Irish population of the whole nation was faced with starvation. This was when the first much larger numbers of immigrants fled their homeland. The majority of this

group went to Canada because fares were very low and ships bringing lumber to England were glad to receive paying passengers instead of returning to Canada empty. As a result of the malnutrition existing among the Irish people, many of them carried typhoid and other diseases.

The potato was the only crop in Ireland during the middle 19th century that was effected with blight. The other crops of wheat, oats, beef, mutton, pork and poultry remained in excellent supply, but were shipped out of Irish ports to the starving Europeans continent for large profit. The memory of ships leaving Irish ports loaded with food while the eyes looking on dimmed was burned into the Irish minds and the stories have persisted through time. It is impossible to erase the vision of ancestors from the emerald isle eating grass to survive.

Throughout the famine years, which continued beyond 1847, the

English bureaucracy was reluctant to appropriate any money to Ireland the help with the famine because they believed that 'the Irish will use it only to buy guns to revolt again.' They did not provide aid in the form of soup kitchens because 'the Irish would get used to handouts and never be self-sufficient.'

The situation was so desperate that the offer of aid came from the Americans to send food directly to Ireland. The English accepted this offer, but only if the ships could land in England first in order to keep the shipping interest fully employed. This action was taken badly by the Americans who pressured for the food not to be diverted under such grievous conditions. The English relented, under world opinion, and the ships sailed directly into Ireland.

It is estimated that one and a half million died of starvation and disease in the Great Famine. Another million people emigrated to Canada and the United States. This caused extreme bitterness among the Irish remaining at home and those that left. The great majority never lost their love for the land. They created stories and songs to engender their patriotic sense of belonging.

Many of the stories were passed down as from the time of the Druids, the Vikings, the advent of Christianity, and the various insurrections over a vast amount of years. People talked about the 'Forgotten Famine' which occurred before the catastrophe of 1845. It was told that the Great Famine was a collection of the events that happened in the first quarter of that century. In 1821 the potato crops had failed in Ireland making unemployment and hunger an everyday problem. Eviction by absentee landlords made for subdivision of tenant property and greater rent. These evictions together with tithes due, the famine and the ongoing religious problems, brought about a critical state in Ireland by 1823.

In the timeframe of the early 1800s, there was a plan by the English government to assist in the emigration of certain Irish families, which gave rise to the first wave of immigrants to Canada. Between the 'Forgotten Famine' and the 'Great Famine' over a million of Irish graced the shores of North America. Some never looked back, but the great majorities keep their country deep in their hearts and endeavoured to assist in any way they could.

Chapter 8

Although life in Ireland was cruel, immigrating to America was not a joyful event. It was referred to as the 'American Wake' for those people knew that they would never see Ireland again. Those

that pursued the immigration path did so only because they knew their future in Ireland would only be more poverty, disease and oppression. America became their dream. Letters from family and neighbours that had emigrated described America as a land of abundance and urged others to follow them through the 'Golden Door.' These letters were read at social events encouraging the young to join them in this wonderful new country. Consequently, they left on ships that were so crowded, with conditions so terrible, that they were referred to as Coffin Ships.

The cruel lesson of life in America came early and hard. It was a constant battle for survival. They were met at the docks by greedy men enticing them to live at their tenement house and exacting an outrageous fee for their services. They predominately settled in the port city, due to lack of means to move on, worked for unscrupulous tyrants, lived in Almshouses and begged for sustenance on almost every street.

All major cities developed their 'Irish Town' or 'Shanty Town' where the Irish clung together. The Irish were not wanted in America, which was reflected by the ads for employment stating "No Irish Need Apply." They were forced to live in cellars and shanties because they were poor and were considered bad for the neighbourhood. Infant mortality in these conditions was set at nearly 80% in New York City due to the living environment of sickness and early death. They were distinguished by their brogue and dress which provoked ridicule. Their poverty and illiteracy provoked scorn.

Instead of apologising for themselves, they united and took offence. Insult or intimidation was often met with violence. Solidarity was their strength; they helped each other survive city life. They prayed and drank together, sometimes drinking was more predominant. It was their dogged determination to become Americans that led an American newspaper to say, "The Irish have become more American than the Americans."

The Irish arrived at a time of need for America. The country was growing and required men to do the heavy work of building bridges, canals and railroads. It was hard, dangerous work where many were killed or maimed, but desperation drove the need to do the labour. The women worked as chamber maids, cooks and caretakers of children. They were linked in poverty and education to the Blacks and determined to be of the same value, which led to extreme dislike between the two races.

The days of 'No Irish Need Apply' passed. St. Patrick's Day parade replaced violent confrontations giving the Irish acceptance. Large influxes of other nationalities into America shifted the hostility onto the shoulders of the newcomers. Throughout the poverty and subhuman conditions, the Irish tenaciously clung to each other. With their ingenuity for organisation, they were able to gain power and acceptance. They fiercely loved America, fought in her wars, but never gave up their allegiance to Ireland and the knowledge that their homeland would someday be free of oppression and domination. Orestes Brownson, a celebrated convert of Catholicism, stated:"Out of these narrow lanes, dirty streets, damp cellars and suffocating garrets will come forth some of the noblest sons of our country, whom she will delight to own and honour." It took little more than a further century for the Irish-Americans to move from a position of despised to the Oval Office.

Chapter 9

Life seems to go on regardless of the hardships or unbearable conditions. The spirit and the bodies of the Irish people were put to the test in an inestimable way during the first half of the 19th cen-

ONAGER OR PERSIAN WILD ASS

tury. Everything they understood in a humble way was removed from their existence. Their lands, many of their sons and daughters and much more of their freedom, yet their spirit remained intact. Possibly, it remained so because of their deep faith or it was an intrinsic mark of their nature. They suffered slavery, exportation to other lands, starvation, deprivation of simple human rights and most importantly, the loss of their lands and animals. The stalwart of the Irish lay in their love of life, family, faith, land and animals. None could take the faith, but most of the other ingredients were removed from the population.

Even in the harshest extremes, the farmers took great pride in the land and the working animals that provided labour alongside them. They were able to endure their lot in life as long as the existence of the Hobby, the horse, the donkey, the chickens and other animals were there to remind them that this was their country and eventually they would be free.

To the evicted farmers in Kerry, the Hobby's preservation was paramount. He represented, in part, their survival. It was difficult to view the ravished lands and countryside of Kerry after all that had transpired. There were six million Irish remaining on the island with a history of ruination. They had seen everything taken from them including the beast of burden that worked so faithfully on their behalf. As the decline of the population occurred, the need to continue and exist persisted. The failure of the potato crop was a situation that they could not control, but they still had to maintain. That meant keeping warm in the winter and somehow providing the bare necessities for their families. They were able to use the services of the Hobby, where he still abided in much lessened numbers. The people had suffered, but so also did the Hobby. Living in the mountains during these incredible times had not served him well. He suffered from malnutrition and in some instances was injured because of lack of any care. The farmers did not have the wherewithal to cure his maladies, but needed his services to haul the turf and other things to their homes. He had grown in some numbers since the depletion in the Peninsular Wars, but did not reach the population that was sufficient for the need that existed. The result was that he had to work harder than ever therefore joining his human counterparts in the mode of survival.

In many instances, the farmers resorted to the use of the donkey for the same labour requirements that had been performed by the Hobby. The donkey had been introduced into Ireland by tinkers, sword sharpeners and ladies of easy virtue who followed the English army into Ireland after domination. The donkey could be purchased cheaply and was dependable for the needs of the farm-

ers/herders. They were used to bring peat from the bogs, carry seaweed, ploughing and slinging hay, taking milk to the creamery and transporting pigs and sheep to fairs. They were adaptable to carts and could be seen at markets carrying fresh fruit, vegetables and fish. Their numbers were large enough and varied in breed to allow the same security that the Hobby had given the farmers in previous years. The Hobby was still used for the various tasks, but could not be owned by the vast majority of farmers because he was nearly extinct. It was through tender love and need that the Hobby retired to the mountain tops and the donkey continued his task of labour.

Chapter 10

The history of the donkey is not too different to that of the Hobby in that both were adaptable to their environments and both were able to endure the harsh conditions existing in Ireland during the

imposition of foreign domination. It is believed that the Hobby originated in Spain whereas the donkey began in Africa and Asia. The African donkey was found between the Mediterranean coast and the Sahara Desert to the south of the Red Sea. There were two separate species: the Nubian wild ass and the Somali wild ass.
The Asiatic branch of the donkey came from a much larger area stretching from the Red Sea to Northern India and Tibet where the ass had to adapt to different climate, terrain and altitude. Consequently, there is more than one type of Asiatic wild ass. The further east the ass was found, the larger, heavier and stronger the animal became. Many of the original breed of those times are now extinct due to the cross breeding and the decline of the use of the donkey, particularly in the Western World.

Donkeys were among the draught animals used to carry silk from the Pacific Ocean to the Mediterranean along the 'Silk Road' in return for trade goods. The overland route was approximately 6,400km and lasted several years. No single animal completed the entire journey and mixing of breeds occurred as unplanned mating happened en-route. The journey ended in the Mediterranean ports of Greece, Italy and the Middle East and Alexandria in Egypt. In Greece, donkeys were found to be ideal animals for working on the narrow paths between the vines. Their use for cultivation in vineyards spread through the Mediterranean countries to Spain, whose coast at the southern tip is separated form north Africa by only a few miles-possibly another entry route for the African wild ass. Again, the donkey and the Hobby could have a

history of heritage in common in their tracings back to Spain.
It is not known if the Hobby was introduced to Ireland by the Spanish or at a much earlier time as was the case with the donkey. The Roman Army was responsible for the movement of donkeys into Northern Europe. Donkeys were used in agriculture and as pack animals as was the Hobby. The donkey came to England with the Roman invasion of Britain in 43AD. They were ignored and forgotten for 1500 years until they were needed to assist man during war. They, along with the Hobby, were used and depleted in great numbers during England's many campaigns throughout Europe.

Chapter 11

The hard times in Ireland, the advent of English control of the land in the middle of the 1840's and then the Great Famine, drove the Irish people to continuous movements that would eventually insure their freedom. All of the previous rebellions had been met swiftly and without mercy. Again, on St. Patrick's Day in 1858, two men James Stephens and Thomas Clark Luby started the Fenian organisation as the Irish Republican Brotherhood. The origin of the term Fenian came from folklore. It described an ancient group of Knights who were self-reliant and had a passion for Irish land. So great was their ardour according to the legend, they gave up a chance for world domination to keep Ireland. This theory fit closely with the beliefs of the modern movement and was taken as the name of the organisation.

The Fenian movement was simultaneously started in Ireland and the United States. The action was largely unsuccessful in Ireland and was clamped down quickly by the English to stop the problem. However, the leaders and members of the group did manage to get the attention of Parliament to focus for a short time on the 'Irish problems.' This was a major step in the forward action for the freedom and separation of Ireland.

In the United States the organisation continued to grow quickly.

Many of the American members gained military experience during the American Civil War and were becoming a force to be feared. Rumours spread that the American Fenians were going to invade Canada, gain control and hold it in ransom for the freedom of Ireland. Initially, the efforts were somewhat successful, but were tempered by the American government when they stepped in to stop the raids.

Seamus McManus, author of 'Story of the Irish Race' wrote that the withdrawal of the American government's support dealt a serious blow to the movement. He described that "The invasion of Canada, which would undoubtedly have been a successful move, and a severe blow to England, was stopped by the unexpected action of the American Government, which, having tacitly encouraged the scheme, and permitted the plans to be ripened, stepped in at the last moment to prevent it."

Had it not been for this American assistance to the English cause, the raids might have been successful and the history of Canada could have been quite different. Some believe that it was the threat of the Fenians, which contributed, to the change of the union of provinces into the confederation that became Canada.

The love of their country allowed the men and women of Ireland to continue the quest for unity and freedom. The Fenians were defeated on both sides of the Atlantic, but this movement passed on the flame of liberty to the next generation. It was in following the tradition of their forebearers, that men like Michael Collins and his generation, forged ahead and gained freedom and independence for their beloved island.

The examples of the French Revolution and the American Revolution set the stage for the continuous struggle for freedom and goal for Home Rule. From the 1870s the idea of Home Rule assumed a leading place in Irish politics. In England, Gladstone attempted to resolve the Irish question with a Home Rule Bill, which he formally introduced in 1886. Following the defeat of Gladstone's second bill, the impetus for Home Rule faded. Throughout the 1890s and 1900s a new cultural nationalism emerged. In 1902 the Irish political leader and journalist Arthur Griffith formed the nucleus of Sinn Fein, which became a political party in 1905. Griffith's original aspiration was for Ireland to become an equal partner with Britain in a dual monarchy, with emphasis on the importance of economic and cultural self-reliance. The name Sinn Fein roughly translated as 'ourselves alone.' By 1918, however, Sinn Fein had absorbed a more radical set of nationalist republicans, and had eclipsed the Irish Parliamentary Party as the most important nationalist party in the country.

Chapter 12

The ever-consuming desire for independence and the refusal to be defeated, prompted the English to introduce measures that might mitigate the pressure of Home Rule and appease the population of Ireland. In the years from 1869 to 1909 a revolution took place in

land ownership in Ireland. Until 1869 Irish farmers rented their farms from landlords. Mostly, they were tenants-at-will who held their farms under a verbal agreement, which could be ended, on either side by six months notice. A minority were leaseholders. Many tenants lacked security of tenure and were vulnerable to eviction during agricultural depression.

The process of land transferral began with the Disestablishment Act of 1869. The main purpose of the act was to bring state support for the Church of Ireland to an end. The problem of how to deal with tenants on church land was solved by granting state loans to buy out their holdings. Only 6,000 did so because most did not have the means to purchase. Large-scale loans to Irish tenant-farmers were not part of the plan in 1869.

In the Land Act of 1870 further steps were taken to allow greater acquisition power giving two-thirds of the purchase price as a loan to buy out the holdings. Again, in 1881 another Land Act was introduced, but the people were very poor and could not afford the terms of the offer. Little more than 1,500 Irish tenants availed of the opportunity.

With the change of political power in England shifting from the Liberals in 1885 to the Conservatives, additional measures were taken to enhance to buying ability of the Irish tenant farmers. It was the Conservatives who introduced land purchase on a major scale. They were a minority government and needed the support of the Irish Home Rule Party in parliament. They hoped that Robert Parnell would urge the Irish people in Britain to vote Conservative in the next general election.

As a result, large amounts of loan money were made available in the Ashbourne Land Act of 1885 allowing for a further 25,000 farmers to purchase their land. Under the previous land acts there was no compulsory clause, which would ensure that the landlords and tenants would or could conclude any purchase. Differences were ironed out with every succeeding Land Act. Each of the

Balfour Act, Wyndham Act and eventually the Birrell Act enacted enough change to enable large-scale purchase with generous payment terms. By 1909 over 390,000 farms had been purchased. Landlord power had been removed but certain factors remained the same. The existing inequitable system of land distribution was perpetuated. Farmers who had previously rented large farms bought out their large farms; small farmers continued to farm the same few acres; a landless labourer was still landless. It had been hoped that giving back the land to the people would kill the demand for Home Rule. The policy was popular among the more-entitled farmers and the landlords. Discontent still was prevalent in the disadvantaged and poor. Author and playwright, John B. Keane sums up the feeling of the time in his play "The Field." The sense of dispossession was set and exposed in the play when the major character is outbid for his rented field resulting in violence and tragedy. The return of the land to the tenant farmers did not accomplish its main objective. The privileged were somewhat satiated, but the majority remained dissatisfied.

Chapter 13

For some the fire was dampened and for others it was extinguished completely. The benevolence of the English government in the return of the land to the Irish people was a magnanimous gesture that was greeted with a diminishing spirit of rebellion in some areas and a burning fervour in others. The large to medium size farmers were able to get on with the labour of life with a great degree of satisfaction and a renewed faith that all would be well under the present system of rule by England. They were in the minority. The desire for Home Rule was still bright in the minds of the majority. The advent of the twentieth century brought little relief from the poverty and misery of the previous century for the poor. They were left with the stories of loss. They had the constant reminders of what had befallen their brothers and sisters in the rebellions and failures of the recent experiences. It was good that the system under the landlords was a thing of the past, but not enough. There are the stories that fuel contentment and those that promote discord. The importance of remembering the good things was always placed in high priority because desperation could overcome the nature. The poorer the area, the more the people clung to times gone by and immortalised events however small or insufficient they may seem to an outsider.

It was difficult to walk the countryside of Kerry without remembering the fables of the wonderful ponies and the people that worked alongside them in all conditions. Each county had their story of malcontent and deprivation, but some places, more than others, promoted the tales of wonder that kept the spirit alive and the body working. Kerry was an example of one of these impoverished counties. There they perpetuated the story of the Hobby, which enabled the soul to endure. Over and over, the Hobby got stronger, braver and endured more than feasibly, any animal would have been able to. His sure-footedness, loving appearance, gentle nature and willingness to work endless hours fuelled the imagination of children and brought tears of regret to those that were privileged to own one of these faithful creatures.

Occasionally, one of the farmers was sure that he had seen a Hobby roaming the mountainside or grazing in the bog. His observation was met with gratitude and thankfulness. Too many years had elapsed since the Hobby had been used and it was reassuring that he could have survived the famine and the lack of care necessary to insure existence. A glimpse of a Hobby reinforced the stories of his being, leaving the hope that he might have subsisted. It was tacitly understood that his numbers were very small, almost extinct. His spirit and the stories remained to remind the people of the time when his numbers were plentiful. It was not in the nature of the Irish to eliminate something for all time. They believed that the Hobby was alive and could multiply again. He was referred to at the hearths as the 'old pony.' His history was rich and his place in the heart was secure. It was not an unusual sight for a farmer, child or visitor to take an extra few moments on the mountain in the hope of seeing a surviving Hobby. He symbolised loyalty, faith and endurance.

Chapter 14

All of the events of the past centuries fuelled the need for independence. The defeat of Home Rule, immigration, starvation, the unfair land acts and the egregious labour practices embittered the people into continuing to form strategies for revolt. The Fenian movement in America helped to provide the training and arms to allow the Irish Republican Brotherhood to instruct and create an army stable and prepared enough to mount the attack later known as the Easter Rising.

Thomas Clarke was the main instigator of the Rising, supported by Pearse, Sean Mac Diarmada, Eamon Ceant and Sean O'Ceallaigh who implored America for further assistance. These men were members of the Supreme Council leading the direction of the rising. Later, Thomas McDonagh, Joseph Plunket and James Connolly were brought onto the Council. James Connolly had been involved in the labour movement in America before starting a similar situation in Ireland.

He emphasised the need for reform and revolt in his many publications such as 'Erin's Hope', 'The End & The Means', 'Socialism Made Easy', 'Labour in Irish History', 'The Irish Worker' and several others. He commanded the Citizen Army during the Easter Rising and was a signatory of the Proclamation of the Irish

Republic. He fought in the GPO and was severely wounded and later summarily executed while strapped to a chair.
The seizure of arms coming from Germany under the direction of Roger Casement was a severe blow to the movement. Other set-backs included the capture of Austin Stack, commandant of the Kerry Brigade and the discovery of the plans for an uprising following a raid on German officials in New York.
The Supreme Council decided unanimously to proceed with the uprising despite the fact that they knew it had little chance of success. It was determined to strike on Easter Monday, 24th April 1916. After occupying the GPO on that day, the Proclamation of the Republic was read to the large gathering. It is as follows:

POBLACHT NA H EIREANN

THE PROVISIONAL GOVERNMENT

OF THE

IRISH REPUBLIC

TO THE PEOPLE OF IRELAND

IRISHMEN AND IRISHWOMEN: In the name of God and of the dead generations from which she receives her old tradition of nationhood, Ireland, through us, summons her children to her flag and strikes for her freedom.

Having organised and trained her manhood through her secret revolutionary organisation, the Irish Republican Brotherhood, and through her open military organisations, the Irish volunteers and the Irish Citizen Army, having patiently perfected her discipline, having resolutely waited for the right moment to reveal itself, she now seizes that moment, and, supported by her exiled children in America and gallant allies in Europe, but relying in the first on her own strength, she strikes in full confidence of victory.

We declare the right of the people of Ireland to the ownership of Ireland, and to the unfettered control of Irish destinies, to be sovereign and indefeasible. The long usurpation of that right by a foreign people and government has not extinguished the right, nor can it ever be extinguished except by the destruction of the Irish people. In every generation the Irish people have asserted their right to national freedom and sovereignty; six times during the last three hundred years they have asserted it to arms. Standing on that fundamental right and again asserting it in arms in the face of the world, we hereby proclaim the Irish Republic as a Sovereign

Independent State, and we pledge our lives and the lives of our comrades-in-arms to the cause of its freedom, of its welfare, and of its exaltation among the nations.
The Irish Republic is entitled to, and hereby claims, the allegiance of every Irishman and Irishwoman. The Republic guarantees religious and civil liberty, equal rights and equal opportunities to all its citizens, and declares its resolve to pursue the happiness and prosperity of the whole nation and all of its parts, cherishing all of the children of the nation equally and oblivious of the differences carefully fostered by an alien government, which have divided a minority from the majority in the past.
Until our arms have brought the opportune moment for the establishment of a permanent National Government representative of the people of Ireland and elected by the suffrages of all her men and women, the Provisional Government hereby constituted, will administer the civil and military affairs of the Republic in trust for the people.
We place the cause of the Irish Republic under the protection of the Most High God. Whose blessing we invoke upon our arms, and we pray that no one who serves that cause will dishonour it by cowardice, inhumanity, or rapine. In this supreme hour the Irish nation must, by its valour and discipline and by the readiness of its children to sacrifice themselves for the common good, prove itself worthy of the august destiny to which it is called.

Signed on Behalf of the Provisional Government
Thomas J. Clarke,
Sean Mac Diarmada, Thomas MacDonagh,
P.H. Pearse, Eamon Ceannt,
James Connolly, Joseph Plunkett.

All of these men were executed by the British Government for their efforts in trying to secure a free Ireland.

The rising lasted five days and caused over 200 civilian deaths and enormous destruction of property. The failure of the country to rise made it impossible to prevent the arrival of English reinforcements. By Wednesday, the revolutionaries were outnumbered by 20 to 1. The English secured a cordon about Dublin and closed in. They concentrated their attack on the GPO whilst none of the other strongholds came under the same sort of concentrated bombardment.

A gun-ship, the Helga, arrived in Dublin and field-guns were mounted on Trinity College. The effect of the continuous shelling of O'Connell Street virtually destroyed it and the surrounding areas. By Friday, the GPO was engulfed in flames and Pearse gave the order to surrender. Four hundred and fifty people, many civilians, were dead with over two thousand wounded. The City was in ruins with the damage and upwards of three thousand five hundred people were subsequently arrested country-wide including Collins and DeVelera. One thousand five hundred were freed after questioning, one thousand eight hundred were interned without trial in England, and one hundred seventy-one were tried by secret court martial resulting in one hundred seventy convictions. Ninety were sentenced to death, but seventy-five of these sentences were commuted to life imprisonment.

The rising was critical in terms of the overall fight for an Irish Republic. For the first time the masses of the country wanted an end to English rule. Nationalism swept the country, especially as the details of the secret executions became known. Although the rising was unpopular at the time, the execution of fifteen leaders engendered widespread sympathy and evoked strong nationalist feeling throughout the country. In the general election of November 1918 Sinn Fein, although it had not been directly involved, was popularly associated with the rising and largely as a result won seventy-three out of the eighty nationalist seats.

Throughout the year efforts by the British administration to reinforce its authority on the island were met with a sustained campaign of guerrilla activity by the Volunteers, which, under the able leadership of Michael Collins, increasingly became known as the Irish Republican Army. The War of Independence carried on until July 1921, when a ceasefire was called. After some preliminary negotiations between DeValera and Lloyd George, Collins and Griffith headed a delegation to London to discuss the terms of an Anglo-Irish Treaty, marking the culmination of the Irish Revolution.

In December 1920, the British coalition government under the premiership of David Lloyd George passed the Government of Ireland Act, which established two Home Rule parliaments: one for six of the nine counties of Ulster, which became a separate political division of the United Kingdom and the other for the remainder of the island. The new parliament of Northern Ireland was opened by King George V in June 1921, confirming in effect the partition of Ireland. In the south, the continuing hostilities delayed the official implementation of the Act until December 1922.

Chapter 15

Rightly, it would seem that the history of the Irish should have had a serious turning point when the Easter Rising produced most of the results desired...freedom from English rule and control of destiny. Some factions of the society were very displeased with the outcome and consequently, a bitter civil war broke out pitting brother against brother in the belief that all or nothing was a better slogan than taking a large part of the victory and building upon it. The Irish Republican Army was now in direct conflict with the Free State Army for control of the political masses.
The war lasted for a period of two years leaving bitterness and disillusionment among the people. By its ending, it also allowed for the forward movement of the formation of government of the Republic of Ireland. Political parties were formed, defeated and re-elected giving rise to the true running of a country. Perfect or to everyone's description of a wonderful world, maybe not, but nonetheless a functional government capable of making decisions and moving the island forward in a democratic process.
The world, including Ireland had survived two World Wars. The need for rebuilding and nourishing was paramount. In the aftermath of WWII, there was a repeal of the Internal Relations Act and Ireland left the Commonwealth declaring the Republic of

Ireland in the year 1949 for twenty-six counties only. The six counties of Ulster remained in the Commonwealth prompting a campaign by the Irish Republican Army for unification in the years from 1951 to 1962. This, along with many other factors, caused the creation of the Northern Ireland Civil Rights Association in 1967. The root for a united Ireland and equality for the people of the North progressed throughout many stages and brutalities. It escalated in 1972 with Bloody Sunday in Derry during a Civil Right march where 13 civilians were shoot by British paratroopers. Internment without trial, hunger strikes, killing of

British soldiers, arm's smuggling and the imposition of Direct Rule by England in the six northern counties, all provided the impetus to promote in a region a sense of distrust, unrest and hardship. In 1993, the Downing Street Declaration...the British Government accepts the right of the people of Ireland to self-determination...provided for a situation where the Irish Republican Army declared a cease-fire. The cessation of hostility by the IRA remained for two years until the British conservative government refused to allow the political arm of the dissention, Sinn Fein, to join all-party talks on Northern Ireland. This perpetuated until 1997 when the cease-fire resumed and negotiation included all parties in Northern politics. In the year 1998, an initial peace-plan was instituted and voted upon by the people of the North. It became known as 'The Good Friday Agreement' and is still in the process of ironing out the details for peace and joint government between the Unionists and the Republicans...

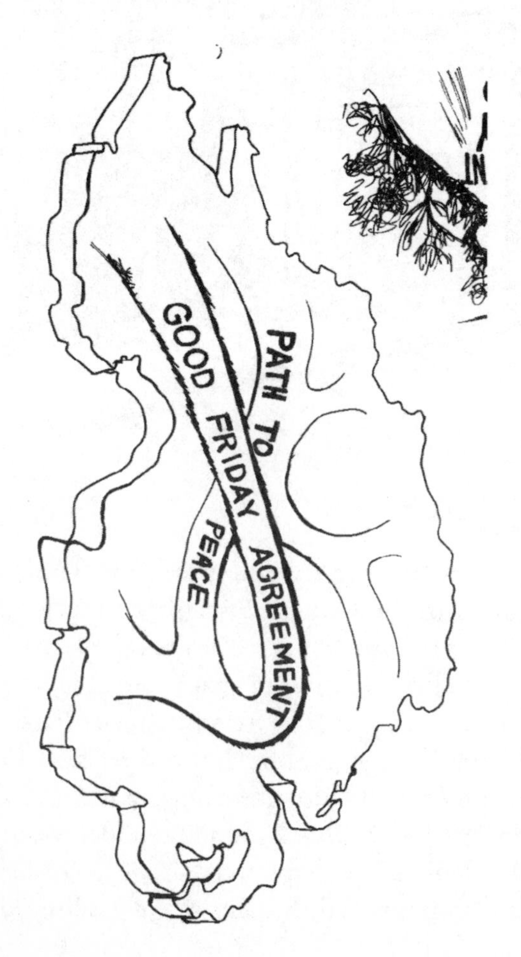

Nothing ever done

between the Irish and the English had a short duration or an easy conclusion. The peaceful culmination of tension in Northern Ireland is the hope of the future in the twenty-first century. The peace process has been halted, restarted, halted and so on. It would appear that history does repeat itself and that prophecy is especially true in Ireland.

Chapter 16

Picking up the pieces was not a strenuous thought process for the ordinary Irish person. It was part of the heritage and custom that had developed over centuries and passed down in storytelling. It was an established fact that the Irish immigrants to America, Australia, England and almost every other part of the world had made their mark on those societies and gained a place in the history books.

They had enveloped trade unions, politics, every known professional occupation and taken their rightful place in the formation and furtherance of those fields. The advantage to make the same in-roads in their own country was not at the disposal of the vast majority of the population. They had the dream, but not the reality until that was won and their future was secure on their native land. Now it was up to them and the prospect was a daunting one. The pieces were those of devastation and ruin. Literacy was non-existent in the masses and hardship was still a thing, which presented a daily challenge.

When the children of Ireland immigrated to foreign lands they did not forget their origins. They remembered by song, desire, story, and to those left behind, a most tangible way. They sent home whatever menial monitory support they could and continued to do so when their means would allow. Many times, this money was the only way survival was insured.

It was not extraordinary then, that the leaders of the new nation of the Republic of Ireland looked to the lands of America, Australia and others for investment into the future of this ancient yet new society. They found most of what they requested and used it to the advantage of the people. They developed an educational system, job markets, entrepreneurial opportunities and a campaign for tourism second to none in the modern world. They invested the time and opportunity and the ingenuity of the people did the rest. New enterprises sprung up in every one of the twenty-six counties allowing for the advent of what became known as 'the Celtic Tiger.' Their entrance in to the European Market triggered additional assistance to the farmers and landholders in rural Ireland. A strategy of involvement in World Affairs gained for Ireland a permanent place on the screen with only progress on the map for the future.

The road to the economic success was paved with pitfalls which had to be overcome. After the Easter Rising and in post-independent Ireland, the elected governments developed fiscal policies that were directed toward to approval of the English government rather than the forward movement of the country as a stable economic entity. Little progress was made in the decades of the 1930s and 1940s. The fledging governments of these times desired to restrain public expenditure and to keep taxation low. This frame of fiscal attitude was motivated to demonstrate that Ireland was capable of fiscal discipline and to facilitate the need to minimise the costs to export industries by low taxation as well as the hope that Anglo-Irish capital would remain in the country.

By the 1950s there was an important change in the framework of fiscal policy. Popular demand for consumer and capital goods, as a result of the rationing during WWII was strong and in those years the government recognised its responsibility to promote by an enlightened budget and investment policy, the continuous use of natural resources of men and material. This change was demonstrated in the idea that capital expenditure was now to be financed by borrowing rather than current, collected revenue. It was believed that the huge numbers of immigrating Irish and the ever-rising unemployment in the country caused a missed opportunity for the government to avail of significant changes.

The depression of the fifties meant that something had to change. Fiscal policy underwent a metamorphosis due to Whitaker's 'Economic Development,' a landmark in Irish economic history. This document recommended tax relief to encourage foreign companies to Ireland, the abolition of tariffs and the embrace of free trade. Significantly, it recognised that fiscal rectitude alone wasn't adequate anymore and it recommended productive rather than social expenditure. This policy, adapted, produced high growth over the next fifteen years which resulted in social and productive expenditure rising. In the later years of this period, Ireland's prosperity and growing population put pressure on public expenditure, yet the current balance remained intact. Tariffs fell due to preparation for the EEC, policy of 'Economic Development' and the Anglo-Irish free trade agreement in 1965. The small tax base served to limit the scope of government spending, though this was addressed with the introduction of turnover taxes in 1960 and PAYE in 1963. Consequently, the period saw borrowing on a very small scale.

The attitude of the people and the government had changed to meet the times of a growing society. New approaches to budgetary procedures owe more to Lord Keynes than to any other man in the process. The 'Keynesian revolution' was recognised in Ireland in the 1930s but not fully embraced until the mid 1970s. The government was determined to compensate for the massive under spending of the previous years and did so by public service job creation and an increase in capital expenditure. Indirect taxes were cut, while lower interest rates accommodated borrowing. The elements of change depended upon the emergence of acceptance of the theory that the burden of public debt suggests that the burden of the debt be shifted from the present taxpayer to the shoulders of the future taxpayers. Fiscal responsibility had emerged to accept the reality of borrowing in the lean times to facilitate need and reduction of deficit in the surplus and affluent periods.

Through trial and error did the nation of Ireland come into its own in the economic world. By developing free and open trade, freeing other aspects of its economy by lowering taxes, decreasing regulation, maintaining low inflation and providing a stable fiscal environment has Ireland been able to grow rapidly enough to surpass Europe's standard of living. The country is managing the balance between the rules and regulations of the European Market and its enterprise friends in other parts of the world. It has come through one of the most successful booms in the history of economic development in the modern world, the 'Celtic Tiger' era and managed to maintain stability in the post period.

World events produce change and force transition to cope with entry into the universal stage. Globalisation, environmental and climate change, traffic congestion, housing needs, immigration and poverty and prosperity become keywords for consideration and involvement. As important as the role of government, fiscal policy and world interaction is, the role of the Irish person is still paramount in the furtherance and development of the homeland. Private entrepreneurs and individual investment of the Irish people have influenced the outcome of the land as much as the dramatic changes. The spirit and love of this island is still the driving force that illuminates and sparks the wonder of the natives and the world.

Chapter 17

In some parts of Ireland the boom in the economy was much slower to have the same import as in the cities and larger towns. The county of the Kerry Bog Pony was one such of these disadvantaged

Picture of the Ring of Kerry … Killarney-Kenmare
Pic: Michael Diggin

spots. There was little to recommend Kerry as an ideal location to situate enterprises mainly because of site and availability to the hub of the country. It was incumbent upon the people in this area to adapt in other ways. This was not easily accomplished.

The wild, rugged beauty of the landscape was the greatest asset that Kerrymen possessed. Early in the development of the eco-

nomic advancement nationwide there were individuals that summoned the world to recognise the qualities of making Kerry their destination for holiday and business conferences. The large towns of Tralee, Listowel, Kenmare and Killarney set about to promote themselves as the ideal location for families, businesses and people of choice.

The idea of the Ring of Kerry became a dominant must for travel to view the landscape of Kerry with its incredible range of mountains, flora and visions to please the entire senses of people not just the sight. Bus tours were established promoting business for the hotels, restaurants and pubs along the route. Private individuals insured their livelihoods by providing the traveller with sights and experiences not seen in other places. One such person, Michael Clifford (better known by his nickname Mike Scart) displayed his unique talent for showmanship by training dogs, goats and poultry to sit upon the back of a donkey while he told stories of the 'old times' in Ireland. It was an incredible attraction and the vast majority of the people touring the Ring of Kerry stopped and marvelled at the talent of the man with the red beard and the animals that would do anything he requested of them.

Adventurers took the place of the downtrodden in the development of schemes that would bring Kerry into the same prosperity that a large part of the country was experiencing. In one of the larger-small towns in Kerry, Killorglin, a businessman promoted an idea into a multi-national commerce with a simple concept. He gathered a group of individuals to embrace the theory of a tax-back system which became approved by the government. From there, the evident benefits to tourists from other parts of the world were realised. The system gave back to travellers the tax that they had paid on items purchased in Ireland when they left the country. This created a wonderful sense of good-will and evolved into a corporation that provided a great deal of employment in Killorglin. It encouraged tourists to return to a country that not

Town of Killorglin, River Luane
Pic: Michael Diggin

only treated them fairly, but was unbelievably beautiful and hospitable.

The town of Killorglin had long made its mark of the physique of Kerry in the annual festival of 'Puck Fair' which is celebrated in the month of August on the 11th, 12th and 13th. There are various legends that suggest the origin for the Fair, many of which are wildly inventive, but it can be reasonable

traced back to a charter from 1603 by granting legal status to the existing fair in Killorglin. The origin of King Puck has a wide variety of stories that relate to the reason for his reverence throughout the centuries. His appearance and that of the Fair have been somewhat lost in the midst of antiquity but the festival survived. Whatever the origin, the fair has long been and continues to be the main social, economic and cultural event in the Killorglin Calendar. It is a time when old friends meet, new friendships are forged and the cares of everyday living are put on hold.

It was decided to celebrate the creativeness of the people of Ireland in the works of writing. Another inventive group of individuals capitalised on the concept and created a writers week that blossomed into an international event. Listowel is the home of many great writers, notably John B. Keane, one of the promoters of writing and its furtherance of the youth of the country. This notion of drawing together the talent of the country and the world allowed for the development of many other interests providing Listowel with a thriving and productive place to live and visit.

The largest town of Kerry, Tralee, again put the thinking cap on and cultivated an ever-growing audience in augmenting a beauty contest called 'The Rose of Tralee.' Each year, young women come from almost every corner of the world to attempt to win the crown and be the receiver of the presentation of a rendition of the 'Rose of Tralee' song. The town is flooded with visitors and the work done on the additional amenities is a testament to the ingenuity of a people wishing to further and enhance their community. The size and availability of man-power for industry was another of the advantages of Tralee. In a short time frame, Tralee hosted a variety of beneficial and lucrative enterprises. The town grew rapidly creating a centre for building, culture, arts and progressed into a thriving society to place one's future.

The Lakes of Killarney was the focal point for the development of the town, along with the incredible mountain range that expounds on the prestige of having the highest peak in Ireland and the

British Isles, Carrantuohill, part of MacGillycuddy's Reeks. This peak overlooks some of the most beautiful scenery. It allowes for a campaign of tourism that pleases the senses in a wide variety of ways. The development of hotels, guest houses, riding facilities, theatre, nature walks, mountain treks, pubs and entertainment bringing back visitors on a regular basis. The hospitality and gracefulness of the people is the first enticement while the services offered insure a return visit. Many private and public corporations have made their headquarters in this beautiful town, which only furthers the lure of the local and international interests.

It is Killarney that starts the voyage on the Ring of Kerry while it winds through the villages, valleys and mountains of the county and terminates in Kenmare. In its journey many agreeable places are encountered and become part of the reason for the success of the notion of the Ring of Kerry.

One of these villages en route is the charming place of Glenbeigh. It is nestled between mountains with the warming breeze of the

Glenbeigh Village
Pic: Michael Diggin

Atlantic Ocean to lure the holiday maker into a feeling of complete satisfaction. Glenbeigh hosts the existence of one of the oldest hotels in Ireland, the Glenbeigh Hotel, and another famed for its cuisine, the Towers Hotel. The rivers Caragh and Behy along with the golf course of Dooks provide visitors with comforts to suit their every wish. The strand of beech at Rossbeigh is visible from every vantage point in Glenbeigh. On a warm summer's night, sipping a pint of Guinness or other in the outside facility of one of the pubs or hotels, the visitor can sometimes hear the lapping of the waves and experience the calming effect of the spirit.
Another of the principal points along the Ring is the town of Cahirsiveen; home to one of Kerry's best fishing ports. It is surrounded by mountains and is bordered on the Atlantic Ocean and Dingle Bay. It is part of the Iveragh Peninsula and has a rich historical, religious and archaeological heritage which is evident in every aspect of the town.
Although not situated on the Ring, the town of Dingle is a place

Iveragh Peninsula/Cahirsiveen
Pic: Michael Diggin

that works its magic most beautifully on the traditional western coast in the heartland of the Gaeltacht where the melodic lilt of the Gaelic tongue is heard in everyday speech. It is said that Dingle is Ireland at its most scenic, with craggy mountains towering over turquoise sea. It is the home of a dolphin named Fungie who frolics around the boats that leave Dingle for trips to the Blasket Islands and Skellig Michael. Vast seabird colonies are present and an amazing century monastery.

As the tour of the Ring winds its way through the mountains and descends in the town of Kenmare, the belief that more beauty and inventiveness could be at the disposal of the traveller is not realistic, but it is so. Kenmare offers many of the same allurements as Tralee, Listowel and Killarney, but with their own flavour. They have developed a community of international interests and compete with enviable relish. Their streets are lined with wonderful shops, hotels, restaurants and pubs. Kenmare provides the traveller with a graceful and calming terminating point for their day journey on the Ring and is one of the spots where people from the globe decide to locate their holiday homes or permanent residence. Kenmare boosts the title, sometimes imposed, as "The Jewel of the Ring."

Kenmare Village
Pic: Michael Diggin

Chapter 18

The county of Kerry can be proud of its accomplishments and it is a reflection of the forward thinking of progressive government that the county was allowed to flourish. Every new idea, new industry and new thought process was given careful consideration and assistance. Town and village councils were aided by the tools put in place by government agencies such as the Tourist Board, Bord Failte and many others. Not only were the more visible opportunities recognised, but also those that would insure the continuance of the heritage and culture of such an ancient society. Appreciation of the bogs, flora, parks, castles, landmark cathedrals and animals that constituted the years of Ireland's development was given the attention that they deserved. There was an attempt to celebrate and conserve those things that made the country and allowed for its development. To forget the past would be to repeat all the errors.

The Kerry Bog Pony was not on a priority list in the scheme of the movement to economic stability in Kerry. The stories were still told of the 'old pony' but more in the thought process that he, like many other things, had lapsed into folklore and extinction. The Hobby, who was the stalwart of the poor farmer, was relegated to a place of storytelling. He was removed from the twenty-first century purely because of the belief that his time had passed and his breed was no longer. His legend did not diminish because of the nature of the people of Kerry. They were not inclined to forget those that had been their helpers and relived every event in their storytelling. They were the innovators of a very progressive society that evolved over the last twenty-five years, had experienced a metamorphosis unequalled in modern times, yet they clung to the old ways preserving what made them unique.

The changes were vast and displayed their effects in a variety of ways. Every devisable method of drawing income into the county was explored and utilised. The scenery was promoted and advertised throughout the world bringing the benefits of tourists and holiday homes into the forefront. The building industry became a booming enterprise providing homes for the influx of foreigners constructing second homes and those that came or stayed in Kerry to make their livelihoods. The towns of Tralee, Listowel, Killarney etc became the hubs of industry and tourism. They became so attractive to the visitor that meetings were held on a regular basis to gage the attractions and those that did not. Investment was placed heavily in the hospitality of the county giving careful thought to preserving while advancing. The parks, mountains, lakes, rivers, guest houses, hotels, riding stables, and every conceivable amenity was scrutinised and a determination was made to improve or change how it effected the overall good of the county. The motivators were constantly looking for new ideas that would make their business distinctive and become a focal point. In addition to the constant green countryside, there had to be other reasons for visitors to come and enjoy Kerry. There was no shortage in the variations of inventiveness that expounded in the later part of the twentieth century and exploded into the twenty-first.

On the now famous, Ring of Kerry, one man John Mulvihill came up with the idea of preserving the tradition of the old houses and ways of the early eighteen hundreds. He felt that this restoration would be informative and a wonderful attraction for the visitor.

He set about recreating structures that told their individual stories. It was important to gather and consult as many people that could make the 'Bog Village' as authentic as possible.

The first house to be built was named for a local man called Jeremiah Mulvihill in order to accommodate Jeremiah and his family in the work of his turf cutting career. Jeremiah's house reveals how the turfcutters of Kerry lived and worked. The lining in the roof is of bog scraw, used because it preserved the heat in winter and maintained the cool in the summer. The floor of the main room had uneven flag stones obtained from the shore or local quarry. The open fire was a constant source of warmth heated by the usage of turf. This chore was the duty of the Hobby and the house summons the memory of the pony that made the drawing and carrying of the peat to the poor houses possible.

Other items that were the constants in the main room of Jeremiah's dwelling and provided the day to day necessities for liv-

JEREMIAH'S COTTAGE

ing were the clock, sleans, pikes, old dresser, and a bench. This house had only two rooms, one for living and one for sleeping. It is not difficult to see the poverty that existed when glancing at the scarce items that made up the everyday essentials of life.

In the second room there was a small bedroom with an old iron bed and a wooden horse for drying clothes or hanging the underwear. There was a lantern, rocking cot, earthenware hot water bottle and the Po under the bed to relieve the need to go out into the night when nature called.

Legend tells the story of Jeremiah and his work of providing turf for many in the surrounding villages and towns. The local village of Glenbeigh and the town of Killorglin were the main focus of his trade. There was ample requirement for the turf. The transport was done by the Hobby and the donkey. Jeremiah realised that his animals needed tending by a blacksmith. On a day in Killorglin, the home of Puck Fair, he met Jack Bell O' Sullivan, a blacksmith. Jack

JACK BELL-

was originally from the town of Cahirsiveen and was known as a great character, an animal lover and an excellent blacksmith. Jeremiah convinced Jack and his family to locate in Glenbeigh. The replica of the forge that Jack Bell O'Sullivan worked is represented as the second dwelling in the Bog Village. The forge has two small windows in order to allow limited light into the room so the blacksmith could see if his horseshoe was red or white. The big bellows is a functioning unit in the house and most of the old fittings, trappings, mill hooves and sides are also present. The floor is replicated in the cobble stone effect while the walls of the forge are thick and strong. The thickness and strength of the walls and a centre section of loose stone was necessary to allow the steam from the hot shoe to escape and keep the forge ventilated.
The need for milk, cream, butter, etc became the deciding factor in the development of the third house erected in the Bog Village. The house of Phil McGillycuddy represented this requirement.

Phil McGillycuddy House

Because of the type of house needed, it is quite different from the first two dwellings. Half of the house was used to domicile the animals while the other half belonged to the farmer and his family. Phil's house was built with a raised back door to accommodate sweeping out the droppings from the cows and ponies at night. To keep the chill from invading the small edifice, a sack was placed against the door. One of the breeds of cow that was kept at Phil's house was the all black Kerry, who was very domesticated, knowing when to come in or go out. Like the Hobby, the Kerry cow was dependable and loving. They were the stalwarts of necessity and loyal friends of the family.
The other items that were used by Phil is the grain crusher which consists of two stones, one with rougher edges than the other, old brooms, butter pats, sacks thrown over the rafters and the wooden

Denny's house

chimneys with open fire places. The men of the times wore hobnail boots which had leather thongs. These boots were heavy and had a good grip when working in the bog or doing other manual work. The more commonly known Wellingtons were not a part of the wardrobe of this timeframe, but gradually replaced the hobnail boots in future generations.

Memories were as important then as now and they were represented in Phil's house by pictures of old times and people. The luxury of telling time found its place in the Fallers clock that originated in Galway and was present on the wall of Phil's humble dwelling.

A ready dietary supplement to the dairy products that came from Phil's house was the construction of Denny's hen house with a back garden for potatoes, cabbage, carrots, onions etc. The people that utilised Denny's hen house were very good gardeners. This allowed for self-sufficiency with little need for the currency of money. The soil had a major quantity of peat content allowing for the vegetables to grow well.

The hen house was not thatched with reed, but made of straw from the sand dunes. There was no intricacy involved in the making of this structure, just a good quantity of straw tied down with stones to prevent it from blowing off. This type of roof had to be replaced every two years.

Denny was a very good farmer and kept a fine flock of hens and chickens. As the village developed, there surfaced a need for someone to do the mundane tasks that would assist the other dwellers in addition to maintaining and running the hen house. That man was Denny Riordan. He was the modern day equivalent of the handyman. He would help in the bog, held horses for the blacksmith and perform whatever tasks required of him. Denny Riordan's house was built simply by the villagers in return for labour received from him. It was a poor dwelling, called 'the Labourer's Cottage', with a mud floor, very few eating utensils and a chimney that demanded little maintenance. The cottage was built in a very basic way so it would need minimum upkeep.

In most villages, there were few labourers. The majority of families were able to sustain without additional help. A man, such as Denny Riordan, was dependent upon the call to work rather than acting on his own initiative. Unlike the reputation of his fellow labourers, that of sullenness, Denny was rigorous and diligent in performing jobs set out for him. As a result, his expertise and experience stood well for him and his reputation kept him in high demand.

The sixth and final house represented in the Bog Village replication is the 'Thatcher's Dwelling.' This house belonged to a local man from Caragh Lake named Paddy Brown. The expertise of

Thatcher's Dwelling

thatching was passed from generation to generation and was a gift not possessed by the larger population. Some people tried to thatch their own roofs, but when a superior job was required, Paddy Brown was called. He was in great demand because of his skill.

In the Thatcher's Dwelling, Paddy laid out the better amenities available in the time. He was a tradesman and his house reflected his position in the community. The house had an upstairs with two beds, the cottage had two lights and the furniture was of better quality.

Walking through the Bog Village and reading the bits and pieces available of the life and times of Jeremiah Mulvihill, Jack Bell O'Sullivan, Phil McGillycuddy, Denny Riordan and his hens and Paddy Brown, it is almost possible to go back three centuries and imaging what life was like. The vegetables, the turf, the Kerry Bog Pony, the fireplaces, the old carts and the atmosphere recreated are mesmerising. The Bog Village, a vision of one forward thinking man and his family, is an institution of remembrance for those that wish to take a journey back in time.

Chapter 19

'All work and no play' was not a circumstance that existed in the Kerry Bog Village of the 1800s or in the present climate in Ireland. Leisure time was as important then as now and the role of sport was a dominant feature of that time The replica of the football pitch in the Bog Village can be seen throughout the countryside of

Kerry centring upon the continuance of Gaelic games and the involvement of the population. Football and hurling hold a prominent place in modern day, but not because the amenities for play are more alluring now. There was no radio, television, news coverage or the ways and means to announce a game...all the same the local people came and enjoyed the match bringing the families for a day out. The same or similar glimpses can be seen on a football or hurling Sunday in the year 2004.

After the game, men settled down to the work of throwing horseshoes while the women talked and the children played. This activity, of horseshoes survived the test of time and is still represented at many of the fairs and gatherings. Of course, the work of talking will never find a conclusion as long as people allow some time for leisure to enjoy themselves. When there is an opportunity to relax and forget the labour of the week, engage in understanding and knowledge and watch the children without worry, the years can roll away and the peace of the Bog Village can be realised.

It is in these moments that history is relived and the pressing events of modern life are discussed. It is sometimes hard to see the present day for what it is. Some things are very clear while others are obscure. The Irish people realise that the 20th century began the great hope that the world would be a brighter and happier place in which to live. In Ireland, the population is the best fed, best housed, and best educated generation ever to have lived in the Western World. To offset all the brilliant accomplishments there are great fears. The society, as previously known, has been uprooted and the pattern of living and behaviour has changed dramatically. Many of the old sign-posts are disappearing and old loyalties questioned. The secular age is upon Ireland giving rise to the loss of meaning, loneliness, aloneness, crime, individualism, family and community. The balance has shifted into a global economy and it has significantly shaped Ireland into believing that the measure for success is in the monetary sense. This has created as much fear as hope indicating that the general consensus among the population is that commerce does not necessarily bring peace. Awareness of the pressing issues in the atmosphere of the island is the immediate response to adapt to the circumstances before the magnitude makes alteration impossible. While this is a huge challenge there are clear indications that whereas the twentieth century has been a time of great material success in the West, the next century and the new millennium could see a major return to things of the spirit. There are signs that the response could come through institutions working in partnership with one another and with the local communities.

Each generation experiences its own trials and tribulations, but can learn and grow by allowing the good of the past to persist while releasing to obscurity those things that were unhealthy for the general populace. The Bog Village reminds the local people where they came from and just how far they have travelled. In homes, at social events and in everyday conversation, there are reminders of the past and their links to the present. Many places, such as the Bog Village, have sprung up all over Ireland allowing for an ancient memory to become a modern guide. Take all that was good and beneficial and leave all that was detrimental and harmful.

The Child of St. Patrick

Overpowered and suppressed
Dominated by an unrelenting nation
Resistance is crushed
Is this the Child of St. Patrick?

Slavery of mind and body
Hunger and despair constant companions
The will of rebellion composed
Is this the Child of St. Patrick?

The ships of immigration
The starvation of famine
Deprive the soul of hope
Is this the Child of St. Patrick?
The bleeding stops
The bells of freedom sound
Each man has a purpose
Is this the Child of St. Patrick?

The children remain at home
Free to learn and grow
The land and people prosper
Is this the Child of St. Patrick?

The growth cycle is on the move
Education and wealth are possible
The nation is advancing into the world
Is this the Child of St. Patrick?

Greed, corruption and avarice
Become the norm of modern times
The people, the politics, the nation
Is this the Child of St. Patrick?

Daily the storms gather
Over a land possessed by a natural grace
To warn of disaster
Is this the Child of St. Patrick?

The laughter becomes less
The wonder of the people is dampened
The evidence of disintegration of spirit erodes hope
Is this the Child of St. Patrick?

Garnish the faith of the people
Force out the evil in the face of ridicule
Work to restore the beauty and innocence
This is the Child of St. Patrick

Chapter 20

Ideas are sometimes the result of dreams, but more often the realisation of a thing that exists in the conscious or sub-conscious. Many stories circulated about a fuel crisis in the 1940s. During that time a Kerryman became a legend for his incredible strength and his ability to work in the bog unlike any other man then or since. The story of such a man, John Daly became well documented in the Bogland Information Centre at Kilflynn, between Tralee and Listowel and in the Kerry Bog Village. This legend and many other tales of incredible men of Kerry and the animals of times gone by provided the impetus for the search to find out if the Hobby was still in existence or had really passed into obscurity. The Bog Village became a stepping stone in the long and arduous task of tracing the Hobby as he journeyed through the bogs and mountains of Kerry.

Nothing can adequately represent the driving need of some people in a quest to uncover the truth and possibly determine the outcome. Environment, upbringing and personal desire are the main ingredients that promote the answers to vexing questions.

John Mulvihill, his wife and sons built the Bog Village in 1991 with loving care to detail, but there was one missing component. In John's youth and well into his manhood, he lived with the tales of an incredible pony that had allowed his father, Jeremiah and his mother Sadie to make a living providing turf in the Limerick area. Over and over again, until he could tell the story with the same accuracy, he remembered the rental of a yard to store turf brought to Limerick by Jeremiah's brother Danny. On cold, frosty days, the small pony that pulled the cart had a difficult time traversing smooth surfaces. Jeremiah put small pieces of canvas bags under the pony's hoofs which gave the Hobby better traction to pull heavier loads and maintain balance in the winter conditions The pony, brought to Limerick, worked in the city as well as he did

in the countryside. Neither pony nor master were totally content to live in the city and after five years returned to Kerry to raise a family and supply turf to a smaller community. Jeremiah valued his pony for loyalty and endurance. He told and retold his children and friends, the merits of the little ponies and how scarce they were and had become. Jeremiah's belief in the pony was fostered by his father's insistence that the pony was invaluable on a farm. The pony was used to go to town to shop and work in the garden. His numbers were much diminished and most of the hard work he had done in times past was now performed by the big horses. The Draught or the Cob was responsible for use in the meadow, drawing hay, ploughing and the vast majority of the much heavier work.

Jeremiah and Sadie provided a good home in Listowel in the turf business while raising their four children, John, Anne, Joan and

Con. Anne married Paul Nyren and tried her fortune in North Dakota in the United States. They have one daughter.
Joan remained at home in Listowel to raise her family. Joan and her husband Damien Stack became proprietors in the Stack family business of the Arcade Furniture Store which is situated next to the famous pub of the renowned poet and author, John B. Keane. Joan and Damien are married for almost thirty years with the blessing of four children, three daughters, a son and a son-in-law. Their interest in the Hobby was stimulated by the enthusiasm of Joan's brother, John Mulvihill, prompting their curiosity about the 'old pony.' This led to the desire to acquire information on the origins and habits of the Kerry Bog Pony. The research and persistence of knowledge precipitated many of the known facts available with regard to the Hobby. Joan researched in the National Library in Dublin and discovered many books that told some of the story of the journey of the Kerry Bog Pony. She has helped make the Kerry Bog Pony Society grow in knowledge and support. The reinforcement of making the acquaintance of Professor Leo Curran, John Flynn (Weatherbys), Daniel Hutch (Veterinarian) and Michael Del Sa Casas (Rare Breeds Society) has strengthened her commitment and dedication to the preservation of the Hobby.
Con married and took up residence in Ballybunion with his wife Marian nee Keenahan. This gravitation to Ballybunion for Con and his wife was advanced because of the familiarity from childhood. In the 1960s, his father and mother, Jeremiah and Sadie, bought a guesthouse in the East End of Ballybunion which boasts seaside retreats and wonderful golf courses. Con and Marian with their five children are privileged to live on the seaside with a ready supply of salt air and seaweed baths.
John married Olive nee Pierce from Derrico in Ballyduff. Olive comes from a family of five girls and one son. Their two sons Timothy (Tim) and Jeremiah (Jerry) are keen advocates and supporters of the Kerry Bog Pony. Both are members of the Society

and work alongside their father, John, to ensure that the Hobby is relegated to its proper place in heritage.
Tim is the older of the sons and has always enjoyed a great passion for sport ranging from soccer to Gaelic football. Two county medals in the under 15s and 16s and a first place at the county athletics championships for long jump are among the accomplishments. Tim's interest in the Hobby dates back to his fourth year of life and has not waned since. As well as an avid sportsman, he owns and trains Kerry Bog Ponies, conducts the operating business of the Red Fox Inn and Museum in conjunction with his father and maintains an active role in the Kerry Bog Pony Society.
Jerry is still attending school with the goal of achieving a four year degree in art from the Limerick Art College. He has written poetry and loves to paint. Some of his work has received acclaim in their purchase throughout Europe and he hopes to continue these ventures after graduation. His involvement with the Hobby began as a young boy of eight and is very much a conduit to his artistic side. He rode his first Kerry Bog Pony, Kerry Star, almost every day allowing for the time to think and dream. The poem, "Out of the Bog" reflects some of Jerry's thoughts.

Out of the Bog

©Jerry Mulvihill February, 2004-06-02

looking at you now, I marvel at all that you've been through
A life of strain and hardship, that was never for you.
I remember you when I was a child,
Standing elegantly and innately wild.
All day you waited by the men in the bog,
Hooves sunken in the ground of marsh
Never anxious, you stayed, through conditions most harsh

Often we spoke of you when the day became night,
"What a hardy animal" my father used to say
As you lay out of sight.
Quietly you gazed on, from your tiny shelter
Ignoring the aches and pains that you daily endured
Everyday alert, and onward you lured

You worked in the Bog, and on the Beach
You carried us to the village, trotting proudly down the Old Bog Road
Each task meant a heavy load.
And now I watch as you graze the open fields
Still beautiful, elegant and innately wild I see
At last, you are finally free

The Mulvihill family tried their fortunes at various endeavours. They lived in Listowel for twelve years and then moved to the quaint and lovely village of Brosna. After Brosna, they moved and lived in Ballybunion for 16 years before becoming involved in the management and promotion of the western Rod & Reel Motel in Cahirciveen. After three years, the reality of a dream materialised with the building of the Red Fox Inn which was managed by John's mother, Sadie, until 1986. Then John and Olive moved from Cahirciveen to Ballincleve and officially opened the Red Fox Inn and Restaurant.

The introduction of the Kerry Bog Village and reconstruction of a long-ago way of life became a reality in 1991. This venture became the first Bog related tourism project in Ireland and Europe. Advice and consultation was sought from Dr. Catherine O'Connell of the Irish Peat Lands Conservation Trust in County Kildare. Authenticity to detail was carefully and lovingly followed.

Every duplication of the Bog Village houses brought the nagging

Patrick Crushell, Catherine O'Conell and John Mulvihill IPCC 20th Anniversary Celebrations & Celebrating Boglands Launch 2002

sense that something was still lacking. The stories of the ponies haunted the memory and the search for information about their existence or extinction became a priority. The pressures and requirements imposed by the running of a museum, restaurant and pub seemed to overtake the importance of the search and knowledge of the 'old pony' until consciousness was resurrected by reading a book "Discovering Kerry." There he was again, the Kerry Hobby, described as a small shaggy pony. It was then and there that the motivation for discovery of his existence, pro or con, became paramount. John decided to explore the idea, but realised he could not sustain such a detailed task on his own. He set-up a committee to help establish research into the plausibility that some strain of the Hobby had survived.

The first meeting was held at the Red Fox Inn on a Saturday night. Enthusiasm must have been superior because the weather was not in a cooperative mood. The evening was wet and dreary, but a large group of people assembled to discuss the Hobby. Various ideas were analysed, many of which eventually became a reality in the emergence of the Kerry Bog Pony.

The local newspapers became instrumental in broadcasting descriptions of the characteristics of the Hobby and requesting help in locating ponies that matched the criteria. The first points, considered at the meeting, were those of locating ponies that had a certain quality and height. Secondary, was the colours of the ponies. The interest was astronomical. Letters, phone calls and claims of ownership of similar ponies flooded in. One telephone call of particular notice was from Paul Murray, who stated that his stepfather, Jim Doyle, owned a little chestnut stallion. After investigation, it was discovered that this stallion had all or at least most of the characteristics of the Hobby. Despite the age of the stallion, he was striking in appearance, well set head, not too big, short back and powerfully rounded shoulders. His legs were extremely strong, plenty of bone and he possessed a mild, kind temperament. John Mulvihill purchased the stallion and so started the furtherance of the rare breed of pony, the Kerry Bog Pony. A neighbour from the Dooks area in Kerry, Mick Teehan, had a mare, Purple Heather, which he brought for breeding with the stallion. The stallion, however, proved to be a shy breeder and the mating did not work. Fortunately, another stallion, Dempsey, owned by Johnny Courtney of Faha, Killarney (RIP) was discovered and bred with Purple Heather to produce a colt foal eleven months later. The colt possessed all the feathers of the Hobby with his chestnut colour and flaxen main and tail. John's wife, Olive, named the colt Flashy Fox because of his beauty and spirit.

In spite of his breeding shyness, Dempsey became the first registered Kerry Bog Pony with a name adjustment to Bog Man. He was purchased overseas and now resides in Thornapple Farms in Vermilllion, Ohio in the United States. He was followed to America by Old Peat, registered Kerry Bog Pony, and resides with an additional three mares and a colt. Linda and Mike Ashar are the owners of the Thornapple Farms and are avid lovers of horses and ponies. They raise Kerry Bog Ponies, Connemara Ponies and Morgan horses. Linda represents the Kerry Bog Pony Society as the North American Liaison Officer of the Society in Ireland. In the winter of 2004, Thornapple Farms hosted a show which produced further knowledge and acknowledgement of the Hobby. Linda designed and sold for the benefit and furtherance of the Hobby a colouring book with sketches and information on the Kerry Bog Pony also becoming known as the 'Heritage Pony.'

From all the publicity that had been generated in the search for the Hobby, Pat Kenny decided that the Kerry Bog Pony was an issue worth discussing on the airwaves. He contacted John Mulvihill resulting in the additional exposure for the Kerry Bog Pony on the radio show and TV, Kenny Live. When Flashy Fox, John Mulvihill and Pat Kenny met for the first time, Pat made an observation and comment that in many ways summed up the journey of the Hobby. On introduction he stated that he wanted the audience to remain calm and conservative because he didn't want the pony to become upset due to the noise, lights and unfamiliar surroundings. He then stated that his next guest, the Kerry Bog Pony, Flashy Fox was "like Lazarus, back from near death." This comment served as a revelation to people that wished to preserve and revere its past and find a place in the present and future for those that made the passage possible.

In addition to the exposure on the Kenny Live show, the Hobby was receiving national attention through the generosity and interest of many other television shows and newspapers. The Hobby, again Flashy Fox, was asked to appear on Nationwide, presented by Michael Ryan, with a special report from correspondent, Tom

Mc Sweeney. Tom took the viewers into the life, experiences and work of the Hobby not forgetting to reinforce the gentle qualities and work ethic of this small pony.

Mary Kennedy and Marty Whelan, the Open House Show, displayed great notice concerning the survival and revival of the Hobby. Mary spoke with John Mulvihill about the pony and had a long-distance telephone call with Linda Asher in Ohio, USA. The Hobby had made it back and had travelled to foreign countries, but had maintained its endearing features. Mary seemed astonished that Flashy Fox did not refuse her stroking attention and was not unnerved by the lights and surroundings.

David Kavanagh did a video piece for Ear to the Ground on the origins of the Hobby using the Kerry Bog Village Museum as a backdrop on the adventures of the small pony. Although the Hobby's main function in the lean times in Ireland centred upon drawing the turf and seaweed to the homes of the farmers and herders, it was gratifying to visualise the pony's use in the transport of people for religious purposes and those of pleasure.

In 1991, the famous movie star, Julia Roberts and her companion, Jason Patric were on a tour of Ireland in the quest for "a nice life and be able to run around and laugh and have fun" Their exploits in the various parts of Ireland were recorded in the 24th November 1991 issue of the Sunday Independent. Julia was recorded as saying that "the most romantic time was the hour-and-a-half they stayed chatting beside a turf fire in one of the cottages in the Bog Village in Glenbeigh." Olive Mulvihill enjoyed some of that time with Julia and Jason while she insured their comfort. They kicked off their shoes and had a pint while lazily basking in the warmth of the fire. They discussed the attributes of the construction of the houses and Olive relayed her and John's plans to revive a strain of pony that was indigenous to Kerry. They were intrigued by the prospect of a pony that was almost extinct and wished Olive and John well in their pursuit for the Kerry Bog Pony.

Chapter 21

As the first committee defined and redefined the purpose and necessity to identify the existence of the Hobby, local and international newspapers were doing their best to spread the description and plight of the Kerry Bog Ponies. It was a discovery that had to be highlighted and resourced to eliminate falsehood and authenticate the reality of the Hobby. "Race is on to save the bog pony" printed in the European and written by Miriam Lord, Dublin describes the luckiest ponies in Ireland. She indicates that the stallions Old Peat, Flashy Fox and the Bogman have been given the task of saving the ancient breed from the brink of extinction. At one point in her article, June, 1994 she notes that there were considered to be only fifteen Kerry Bog Ponies left. She relates the wonderful conditions that the ponies are kept in and speaks highly of the effort to preserve them. David Coleman of the Chase Journal tells a story in his writing that indicates"chance happenings in this life often lead down strange roads." David goes on to reiterate the path of discovery of the Hobby and then details its cautious return to the land of acknowledgement. In his article, David dons Pat Kenny of the Kenny Live show as the patron saint of the Kerry Bog Pony because of Pat's comment regarding the ponies about Lazarus and rising from the dead.

The Cork Examiner, 3rd March 1998 heads its story "My kingdom for a Kerry Bog Pony." After all the hard work of the Society and other interested parties, journalist Donal Hickey, notes that "the timid, little Kerry Bog Pony is about to take its place among the high and mighty of the equine world." Donal was referring to

Left to Right: Minister Joe Walsh, Deputy John O'Donoghue and John Mulvihill

the fact that the Hobby has been declared a rare breed and will receive a passport which proves pedigree. "Recognition for Kerry Ponies" was the heading for an article written in Ireland's Horse Review in May 2003. Outlined was the distinctive features of the pony, the scientific reports of laboratory testing, and the hope for the eventual export of the Hobby.

Years prior to the pronouncement of pedigree, the Kerry Bog Pony was described and exalted by the Farmers Journal. In this prestigious journal, many of the findings of additional ponies held by owners all over the county were able to contact John Mulvihill and some of the major work of discovery was enabled. The Irish Times was instrumental and gracious in the furtherance of broadcasting information about the Hobby. One of the articles in the Times, 5th April 1994 written by Agriculture Correspondent, Sean Mac Connell reported on the condition of search for the Kerry Bog Pony. His article was headed "On the trail of the Kerry Bog Pony." He reiterates most of previously stated information, but becomes another source to advance the search and knowledge of the Hobby. Another Irish correspondent for the Times, Audrey Magee, headed her article "The bog pony that nearly sank without trace." Her writing gave some explicit information about the discovery, desire and eventual resurgence of the pony. In February 1994, Kerry's Eye Newspaper led their article "Kerry Ponies Best in Ireland" which was the result of a compilation by Russell Mc Morran. The endurance of the Hobby was restated giving credit to the small pony for his ability to endure great burdens while maintaining a gentle nature and sagacity unequalled by any breed. That same year, the Kerryman, written by Catherine Halloran, ran the headline article," Historic Kerry Bog Pony about to make a comeback."

The agricultural minister, Joe Walsh and Deputy John O'Donoghue were among the first official visitors to the Bog Village and discovered an ancient pony that belonged in the annals of Irish/Kerry history. "This pony is bringing the whole heritage of the area back to life." Since then, John O'Donoghue has been the Minister of Justice, Equality and Law and most recently Minister for Arts, Sports and Tourism. In all of his roles in government, he has remained a staunch advocate of the resurgence of the Hobby and has helped in its furtherance.

In 1999, the magazine, Ireland's Equestrian did a cover story with six additional pages dedicated to the story of the Kerry Bog Pony. The first page deals with the pony being saved from extinction while the other pages show the originator of the effort, John Mulvihill and his beloved ponies in the Kerry Bog Village. One of the many quotes in the writing "Despite the tide of popular opinion and ardent expressions of the breed's demise, John Mulvihill persevered in the hope that the greater majority might somehow be mistaken." Mistaken became the password and the Equestrian documents a large part of the proof of a living breed.

Ireland of the Welcomes in their magazine issue of September/October 1995 date the pony back the difficult times in Irish history and relate how the road was made easier by the existence of the Hobby. The article sums up the voyage "This pony is bringing the whole heritage of the area back to life. There is a huge market for it in both Europe and around the world- the world is open to the Bog Pony."

Around the world the pony has been noticed. A German magazine, freizeit im sattel, produced the story of the Kerry Bog Pony in their January, 1997 issue. If knowledge and broadcasting promote understanding and acceptance, then the Hobby has truly found its place in history. It has been by the kind acknowledgement and help of multitudes of people that the pony is grazing and multiplying.

Chapter 22

The work of discovery was greatly enabled by the dedicated efforts of many people. As the publicity of the Hobby became nationwide, attention was drawn to the euthenics of the pony. John Flynn, Weatherbys Ireland, DNA Laboratory, Irish Equine Centre, contacted John Mulvihill in an effort to ascertain the recognition status of the pony by the Irish Horse Board and to recommend that the animals undergo blood typing to prove and differentiate the Hobby from other breeds of small ponies in Ireland.
Weatherbys undertook to establish the Genetic Analysis of the Kerry Bog Pony Population. He elaborated that Ireland has a long tradition in the breeding of horses and ponies spanning many centuries. Both horses and ponies played a vital role in small and large scale farming economies and also provided an essential means of transport. While most breeds were geographically well represented throughout Ireland, some regions were synonymous to particular breeds of pony depending on their size, conformation, adaptation and suitability to a specific area. The most obvious and best known example to fit this category was the Connemara Pony.
John Flynn noted in his observations that there was abundant, historical and anecdotal evidence to prove the existence of another pony breed, indigenous to the south western region of Ireland.

The pony was particularly suitable for the vital role of transporting turf as a form of domestic fuel and became known locally as the Kerry Hobby or the Kerry Bog Pony.

After the initial contact and discussion was started in 1994, Weatherbys conducted a blood typing program on all ponies that fulfilled the criteria in the classification of the Kerry Bog Pony Breed. John Mulvihill's, Flashy Fox was the first Hobby to be blood typed initiating the genetic testing program of qualification. In 1998 The International Society for Animal Genetics (ISAG) changed from blood typing to DNA genotyping. Since then all stallions, brood mares and offspring were again tested using the new protocol.

A total known population of one hundred and fifty-two Kerry Bog Ponies were analysed. In this number there were six stallions, seventy-three dams and their subsequent offspring. A total of twenty-one genetic sites were analysed for the transmission of one-hun-

Irish Horse Board Director General, Dermot Ryan, meets delegates from the Kerry Bog Pony Society. Left to Right: Dermot Ryan, Nora Byrne, John Mulvihill, Daniel Hutch, Joan Mulvihill Stack, Siobhan Flynn, Leo Curran, John Flynn.

dred and twenty-seven identified alleles to provide enough data for a population genetics study of this breed. The alleles were identified using three distinct technologies, namely Allo-Immuno Red Cell Typing, Biochemical Protein Polymorphisms and DNA Dinuleotide Microsatelite fragment analysis.

Based on the extensive investigation conducted by John Flynn at Weatherbys Ireland into the Kerry Bog Pony population at genetic level, some very interesting findings have emerged with regard to the frequency of particular gene variants identified within the breed. Comparatives with four other breeds clearly demonstrate that this population can be considered a pony breed in its own right. John Flynn strongly advised, based on the restricted genetic pool of mares and stallions within this population it is vital that proper breeding management be introduced through studbook registration. Efforts have been made successfully allowing for the qualification of each pony meeting the specific criteria to gain registration which will now guarantee the compilation of the breeding data and tracking of the Hobby in his world of recognition.

Another man extremely instrumental in the process of documenting the Hobby is Dr. Leo Curran. Dr. Curran is one of the founders of the Irish Genetic Resources Conservation Trust LTD. He became involved in the resurgence of the Kerry Bog Pony in an effort to assist in the restoration of the breed. He is the author of "Kerry and Dexter Cattle and other ancient Irish Breeds: A History 1990," "Feara agus Banta Eireann," Toward the History of Agricultural Science in Ireland" and "The Native Lowland sheep of Galway and Roscommon: A history." He became a member of the Kerry Bog Pony Society and is wonderfully supportive in his advice and attendance.

Veterinary Surgeons have been very instrumental in the clarification and descriptions of the Kerry Bog Pony. Timothy Clifford, Killorglin, Co. Kerry verified and documented the size, weight, colour, coat, head, body, legs, probable activities and temperament

of the Kerry Bog Pony. He has been willing and helpful in the genetic testing in accordance with specific guidelines.
Daniel Hutch, M.V.B.,M.R.C.V.S., has put his considerable experience to work in the testing and treatment of the Hobby. He is married to Vanessa with two sons, Sebastian and William. Daniel is the founder of the Troytown Veterinary Hospital and is a third generation veterinary surgeon drawing on a hundred years of professional experience in the Hutch family. His lifetime involvement with horses, both as a practitioner and breeder of thoroughbred racehorses, led him to a passionate interest in bloodlines. After the results of the genetic testing, Daniel Hutch stated "the Kerry Bog Pony has now become an established breed. The rest is history."

Chapter 23

Ordinary folk to do an ordinary job. That was the idea which promoted the think tanks behind the discovery and preservation of the Hobby. In 1994, the original committee formed on that wet, dreary night, consisted of members of the community that had varied and interesting backgrounds. John Mulvihill was unanimous in the position of Chairman of the Kerry Bog Pony Society. He was the impetus that garnished the services of the Assistant Chairperson, Sheamus Fogerty.

Sheamus was a man with strong farming background and an ardent love of the equine world. He was able to promote and encourage the movement of the Hobby through his additional ventures as a couch driver. The secretary, Clare Hoare, came from the Killorglin area assisting her husband in the import and sales of farm and building tractors, diggers and all types of equipment. Her local knowledge of the vicinity and her community spirit was an able asset to the group. Assisting Clare in the paperwork of the Society was Michelle Desmond. Michelle brought a great enthusiasm because of her love of ponies and donkeys from early childhood. Before coming to Kerry, she had riding stables in Dublin where she was given a present of a small pony when she was a child. Unaware of the existence of the Kerry Bog Pony at the time,

Names from left to right:
Peter McWhinney, Ann Pouch, Philip Smith, Mena Sullivan, George Pouch, Carol McEvoy, Tim Dennehy, Joe O'Sullivan, Pat Byrne, Arlene Aston, Sinead Byrne, Norma Cook, John Mulvihill, Michael Teehan Jr., Michael Teehan Sr.
Missing from photo:
Dr. Leo Curran, Mary McGrath, Rachael Sterling, Michelle Desmond, Tim Cooper, Tim Mulvihill.

Michelle gave the small pony to a family in Blessington where he won every pony class in the shows he entered. After moving to Kerry, Michelle visited the Red Fox Inn and rediscovered the Hobby. She purchased a yearling, Brave Badger, in Castlegregory. This again ignited her interest in the small pony, but this time she was aware of the plight of the Hobby. It was then that she decided to help in any way to assist in the recognition and preservation of these outstanding ponies.

John Mulvihill's sister Joan Stack volunteered to do her part for the society by acting as the Treasurer. John Courtney (RIP), Assistant Treasurer, worked with Joan to ensure that the Society would have the funds to initiate the search and discovery of the Hobby. John was a farmer and a lover of animals. To supplement his income in modern times he worked as a lorry driver and encouraged the spread of information about the Kerry Bog Pony.

In order to reach as many ears and centres of knowledge, Robert Donaldson, took on the position as PRO for the Society. Robert is the president of the Irish Miniature Equine Society and has been deeply involved in the promotion of horse and donkey interest for many years. His enthusiasm for equine Breeds has led him over the last years to assemble a stable of pure-bred miniature horses and donkeys, ranging from Shetlands, Falabellas, Kerry Bog Ponies, British international miniatures and Sardinian Miniature Donkeys. His energy and knowledge has been a wonderful asset in the promotion and acknowledgement of the Hobby. Anne Hayes took on the daunting task of assisting Robert in his endeavours as the assistant PRO.

A great deal of the footwork was performed unselfishly and devotedly by the initial officers of the committee. As the years progressed new names and faces became interested and committed to the Hobby and his future. John Mulvihill moved into the position of President of the Kerry Bog Pony Society giving way for Norma Cook to take over the duties of Chairperson. Norma resides in East Blessington, Co. Wicklow, is married and has two children. She took over the management of the family farm of three hundred acres when her father fell ill in 1957. The farm had labourers, and was a mixed enterprise of cereals, a herd of cattle, thoroughbred horses and brood mares. She came in second in the Farm Woman of the Year Competition in the years of 1987 and 1989. Norma deviated from her farming background when she married and moved to Wales. When her two girls started secondary school, Norma returned to Blessington and farming. She became involved in the local branch of the Irish Farmers' Association and was elected Secretary. From there, she and her family built on their background and became involved in the Kerry Bog Pony. Her enthusiasm and dedication is symbolic of her background and she is devoted to keeping this lovely pony alive.

Arlene Aston took on the responsibilities of treasurer in the new committee. She lives in the picturesque Ards Peninsula outside Newtownards, Co. Down and is probably the most Northern Ireland based member of the Kerry Bog Pony Society. She, along with her long-time partner, Peter Mawhinney has been involved with horses and ponies since childhood. They consider riding, competing, showing and most equestrian disciplines a major part of their lifestyle. Arlene's daughter, Andrea has been riding and is a consummate contestant in the sport of show jumping. Their first acquaintance, resulting from an article written in John Mulvihill's words, with the Kerry Bog Pony produced the purchase of a Hobby, Red Vixen and a filly coal, Moneen Colleen. Later, they purchased the stallion, The Spotted Badger. They found the ponies to be pretty, intelligent, inquisitive, loving and sure-footed animals with an affinity to children. In local horse shows, to further promote the Kerry Bog Pony breed, Arlene and Peter have represented their stock for review. Not surprisingly, the behaviour and gentleness of the Hobby remained the same while at the show or grazing in the field.

Another new face and interest in the Hobby is committee secretary, Rachel Sterling. She lives with her husband, three children and many assorted animals outside Nenagh, Co Tipperary. She has a long-time love and association with ponies and is involved with breeding and producing them for show. She has one gelding, which the children ride and drive in a tiny trap, and three mares. She tries to assimilate the conditions that the Kerry Bog Ponies experienced in times long gone by allowing them to herd with visiting mares and a summertime stallion.

Tim Cooper, Droum Head Ford, Killarney, Dr. Leo Curran, Macetown, Tara, Co. Meath, Mary McGrath, Rosetown Lodge, Newbridge, Co Kildare and Tim Mulvihill, Red Fox Inn, Glenbeigh Co. Kerry are the members of the standing committee in recent years. Each brings their special brand of expertise to the forefront in the promotion and care of the Kerry Bog Pony. Tim

Cooper is a dairy farmer with one-hundred acres of mixed land and forestry. His interest in ponies dates back to his youthful days when he worked with them on the farm before modern equipment was available. He purchased his first Kerry Bog Pony as a swap for a donkey at the Newmarket horse fair in Co Cork. After learning from various sources and visiting the Red Fox Inn, he realised that his small pony was a Hobby, Quagmire Prince. The Prince is one of the foundation stallions of the Society and has represented himself well at shows throughout Ireland. He has received ribbons at Kilgarvan, Killorglin, Athy, Tinahealy, Thomastown, Enniskillen, the R.D.S. Dublin show and many more. His foals, tested and qualified, have been exported throughout Ireland, Northern Ireland, England and the United States.

Mary Mc Grath is a descendent of a great line of horse lovers that became acquainted with the Hobby in a natural quest for knowledge about a heritage pony. Her grandfather bought the great Nasrullah from the Aga Khan and won the Epson Derby with Arctic Prince. Her father bred two Derby winners, Oaks and Leymoss, but his greatest love was show jumping. He owned and won the International Grand Prix with Goodbye ridden by Seamus Hayes. Mary was raised on a stud farm where horses were everywhere, stallions, mares, foals, working horses, hunters, show jumpers, ponies and even a white mule. She heard about the Hobby on a radio show and went to see John Mulvihill and the ponies. John sold her two little bay youngsters with white points who were like mountian goats and absolutely adorable. Their personality proved to be very different to any other native breed. They have a sense of fun, are brave, strong, intelligent, have big hearts and are as cute as foxes. Mary believes that the Kerry Bog Ponies are unique and that the future will be a better place if the Hobby lives long and prospers.

The Kerry Bog Pony Society boasts a membership that is growing in strength and knowledge as the years progress. Every member has a story and a reason for his or her love of the 'old pony.' George Pouch, Stephenstown Lodge, Two Mile-House, Naas, Co Kildare and John Bonar from Co. Mayo are but two of the ardent admirers of the Hobby. The fame and fortune of the pony is spreading far and wide within the confines of his native land because of such support.

George purchased a four-year mare in foal from Arlene Aston. The colt, Misty of Allen was born in June, 2004 followed by the purchase of another yearling colt from John Mulvihill, The Bog Badger who is currently one of the foundation stallions of the society. George describes his ponies as possessing uncanny speed and stamina, have a natural jumping ability and are easy to maintain. He believes that they will be wonderful ponies for children and demonstrate unique ability in driving competitions. George fully understands the feeling of achievement in being involved in some small way in saving a part of Irish/Kerry culture.

John Bonar, his wife Mary and four children, Donna, Barry, Michael and Evelyn live in the southern foot hills of Croagh Patrick, Ireland's holy mountain in Mayo. They have a farm consisting mainly of sheep with some foul. They wanted to introduce an added measure to their experience and decided to inquire about an equine. A lot of issues were taken into account before making a determination. They required an animal that suited the farming environment, easy to manage, physically not too large and placid by nature. After meeting John Mulvihill and the Kerry Bog Pony, there was no contest. The decision was easy to make. The pony met all of the criteria, and there was a feeling of accomplishment in helping in a practical way to ensure the survival and revival of this great Irish pony.

There are many people that have been instrumental in the admiration and furtherance of the Kerry Bog Pony that have not told their particular stories. At a meeting of the Society, there is love, dedication, need, longing, but most of all, the driving force to inform, educate and promote the Hobby. Every member and their families have contributed greatly to the Kerry Bog Pony, but it is only his due. The Hobby did more than his share in the lean times and deserves dignity in the good times.

Chapter 24

The time is five o'clock in the morning in the month of May, 2004. A vast variety of birds are chirping, feeding and the cacophony of sound is music to the observer. The mountains are still in the glow of the full moon that is sensing the competition of the rising sun to take its place in lighting up one of the most beautiful places on earth. The place, Kerry, is beyond description on such a morning. The rippling of the ocean and rivers, the changing vegetation on the mountains which provide ecstasy to the eyes, wild flowers, serenity of the bog lands, trees waving gently in the wind, the soothing sounds of the cows, sheep, foul, horses, ponies, donkeys, dogs, cats, and even some people that are early risers, make for a picture that will not and probably could not be put to canvas. It is a total experience, but one that cannot be recalled by the human hand.

The Hobby has taken his place in this scene. He grazes in leisure and without fear of abandonment or extinction. Unselfish effort has traced his origins and his possible beginnings. He was a component in the complexity of the life and history of the people he laboured for and loved by his dedication. He had no voice to request acknowledgement. He could not ask for his qualities to be remembered and furthered. He retreated to the mountains to lick the wounds of centuries and waited for the bell of doom to sound. In the glow of the beautiful morning, there is no ringing of a bell. Only the resounding joy of nature that the addition of a species has been remembered. The Kerry Bog Pony (the Hobby) is home and thriving.

The End of this story, but the beginning of the Hobby.